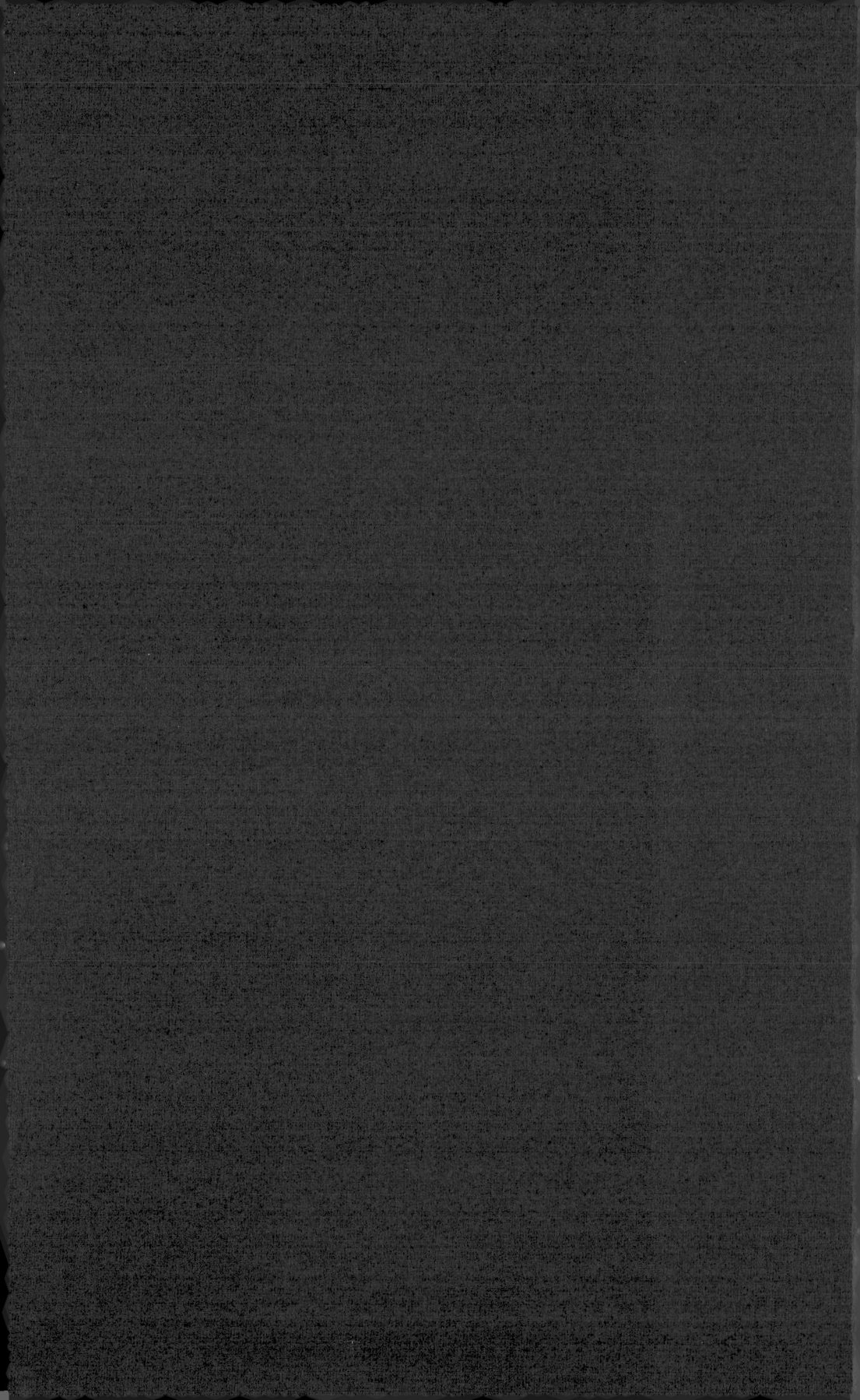

秋言物语

QIU'S MONOGATARI

马小秋

著

社会科学文献出版社
SOCIAL SCIENCES ACADEMIC PRESS (CHINA)

马小秋

鼎益丰集团创始人、总裁，中国鼎益丰控股有限公司非执行董事，深圳市企业联合会副会长，第八届"深圳十大杰出女企业家"。

早年研究西方哲学、美学、中医学的马小秋出生于"天府之国"——四川成都，川人的率真爽朗赋予她与人为善的真诚和对事业孜孜以求的韧劲。20世纪八九十年代，马小秋创办的以健康共享、友善服务为理念的研究机构和公司为她带来了成功，而更多的收获来自做人做事的坚守与责任，同时也渐渐从中体悟企业家精神的养成。

企业家是企业的精神领袖，不仅创造财富，更重要的是具备把自己的思想传达给整个企业的影响力，以自己的价值观去影响企业，影响社会的进步。1999年，马小秋开始研读中华传统经典，研修东方古老智慧，与隋广义先生结识，在亦师亦友的交流中学习和领悟，用传统文化的智慧与精神，为现代企业注入优秀文化基因，以优秀传统文化涵养现代企业家精神。在隋广义先生的影响下，马小秋立志为传播中华传统文化奋斗终生。

2011年，马小秋女士携手隋广义先生，投资创立鼎益丰集团。作为一位优雅的女智者与具有睿智眼光的天使投资人，做人决定做事的方向和高度，做人胸怀宽广、强烈的社会责任感，留有一份历史的标尺和文化的底蕴在心中。

厚德载物，以德治企。在中华优秀传统文化的传承发展中，鼎益丰集团在马小秋的带领下进行了广泛的实践与探索，并创造了具有中国传统文化特色的企业发展之路：全面贯彻"无我、利他、专一、守信"的企业精神，将《道德经》蕴含的传统文化智慧与企业经营管理、人力资源、企业文化建设、品牌市场推广等众多领域密切结合，并总结出"上以无为、下以有为、事以合为、无所不为"的企业管理经验。

在传统文化的滋养下，鼎益丰集团短短八年时间，发展成为一个具有广泛影响力的道德资本、道德文化平台，也是当前少见的用传统文化培植出来的企业典范。在全球化时代的今天，不同文化间的对话交流愈加频繁，相信在中国传统文化与西方理论不断互补融合的未来，鼎益丰集团和马小秋女士所秉持的以中华优秀传统文化支撑企业发展的理念，将走向更大的舞台。

Ms. Ma Xiaoqiu

founder & president of Ding Yifeng Group, non-executive director China Ding Yifeng HK, Vice President of Shenzhen Enterprise Federation, vice president of Shenzhen Wanmingzi Charitable Foundation. In the 1980s, answering the call to Deng Xiaoping "let some people get rich first", went south to build a business. In 2011, she joined hands with Mr. Sui Guangyi to found Ding Yi Feng Group and has practiced the spirit of "Selflessness, Altruism, Singleness and Trustworthiness" in Ding Yi Feng Group, and run a business with culture and morality. On the basis of cultural self-confidence, Chinese wisdom Dao Te Ching is successfully used in enterprise practice to create a wealth model with Shenzhen-style innovation, and to create a culturally self-confident enterprise with nearly 100 billion yuan under its management. She won Woman of the Year Award of American International Chamber of Commerce in 2018 and the Ten Women Entrepreneurs Award of Shenzhen, China.

推荐序

上善若水　嘉言如玉

案头一册《秋言物语》，读之令人醍醐灌顶。

"道，可道，非常道。"道，是宇宙之本原，天地之起始，万物之根，造化之基。《秋言物语》，与道相应，澡雪精神。

儒家大师荀子（战国末年赵国人）曾在楚国教帝王之术，他的弟子韩非子（战国末年韩国人、韩王之子）深谙道学与治术。他在《解老》中说："万物各异理，而道尽稽万物之理，故不得不化；不得不化，故无常操。无常操，是以死生气禀焉，万智斟酌焉，万事废兴焉。天得之以高，地得之以藏，维斗得之以成其威，日月得之以恒其光……道，与尧、舜俱智，与接舆俱狂，与桀、纣俱灭，与汤、武俱昌。以为近乎，游于四极；以为远乎，常在吾侧；以为暗乎，其光昭昭；以为明乎，其物冥冥。而功成天地，和化雷霆；宇内之物，恃之以成。"只有心量广大、犹如虚空的人能体道、悟道。

马小秋女士天赋异禀，言下即悟，深参《清静经》"大道无形，生育天地；大道无情，运行日月；大道无名，长养万物"之理，天地之间，无极而太极，先天元神不动无欲，后天识神动而有欲，必返乎先天，才能天真思诚。禅道究天人之学，不立分别相，不垢不净，不增不减，大道至矣尽矣。更难得的是马小秋女士能将禅道儒

I

三教润泽商道，令人感佩。道家的"道法自然"、儒家的"仁者爱人"、禅宗的"心体无滞"，这三重境界，由心到物，万象森罗，中华文化的圣哲贤者对于人生世相的明哲思辨，跃然纸上。

"古之善为士者，微妙玄通，深不可识。"所谓深者，道也、心也。道在无形，心在空性。马小秋女士天植灵根，体悟极深，谓"道乃空性，涵养万物，无善恶之别"。由道入佛，她对佛教颇有感应。《心经》乃六百卷大般若经的心要，求般若之智，莫若中观，知其味者，甚为稀有。《秋言物语》道："有与无，色与空，动与静，曲与直，明理者当立于非暗非明之中道。"玄之又玄，众妙之门，悲智双运，以心转境，有几人明？中道至难，《论语·庸也》云："中庸之为德也，其至矣乎。"中者，天下之正道、至道也。

空性生万法，亦即心生万法。禅学求心。万法是由缘而起，缘起缘灭，成住毁空。因缘从心而生。心生则万法生，心灭则万法灭。弘忍大师给惠能讲到"应无所住而生其心"的时候，六祖言下大悟：何期自性，本自清净！何期自性，本不生灭！何期自性，本自具足！何期自性，本无动摇！何期自性，能生万法！

儒家讲世间法，世间法最精微处即是心学。明代儒学大师王阳明出入佛老，归宗孔孟，四句教名闻天下。"无善无恶心之体，有善有恶意之动，知善知恶是良知，为善去恶是格物。"心的本体是天理，无一毫私意，如明镜一般，无善无恶，无物不照；心物相接，感而遂通，便有意念，有善恶；心能知道、知天，能觉能照，能知善恶，省察克治；格物即是格心，格其非，以正其心。心学的奥妙，不偏有，不着空，直指人心，直趋中道。

以心照物，乃阳明心学最精髓处。《传习录》有这么一段经典的记载，先生游南镇，一友指岩中花树问曰："天下无心外之物，如此花树在深山中自开自落，于我心亦何相关？"先生曰："你未看此花时，此花与汝心同归于寂；你来看此花时，则此花颜色一时明白起来，便知此花不在你心外。"

知行合一，就是以心照物、心物相照的道理。王阳明曾做了一首诗《咏良知四首示诸生》："人人自有定盘针，万化根源总在心。却笑从前颠倒见，枝枝叶叶外头寻。"心是万化之源，不求心而求物，不求内而求外，离开自心而另寻本源，岂不是颠倒梦想？

《秋言物语》中处处可见觉照之心。治企之道，亦繁亦简，放下小我，成就大我。时时在定，处处在修，心性大放光明。觉照，就是心之光明，就是人性所立之处。人是天地的心。宋儒教人"为天地立心"，正是此意。在《传习录》中，阳明大师与学生友人论道。先生曰："你看这个天地中间，甚么是天地的心？"对曰："尝闻人是天地的心。"曰："人又甚么叫做心？"对曰："只是一个灵明。"《秋言物语》心心念念以"兴业济民"为企业使命，以"无我、利他、专一、守信"为企业精神，就是充天塞地间的这个灵明。有这个心，有这灵识之根，世界就会生生不息。

是为序。

韩望喜

深圳市委宣传部副部长
市政府新闻办主任

PREFACE

Best conduct is as water, best words are as jade

❝ A Collection of Essays by Ma Xiaoqiu" on the desk, it is sobering to read.

❝ Tao can be told of is not the Absolute Tao." Tao is the origin of the universe, the beginning of the heavens and the earth, the root of all things, the foundation of creation. The *Qiu's Monogati* is corresponding to the Tao. Snow bathing and mind cleaning.

The Confucian master Xun Zi once taught the art of emperors in the State of Chu. His disciple Han Fei was deeply versed in Taoism and governance. He said in the *Interpretation of Lao Tzu*: "The Tao is to explain why all things are different and the reason for all things, so it has to be changed. Had to change, so impermanence; the impermanence is based on death, birth and qualities. If a wise man thinks things over, everything will be abandoned or flourish. With the Tao, the Heaven is blessed with great wisdom, the earth has precious deposits, the Big Dipper is powerful and the Sun and the Moon are light forever. Tao is as wise as Yao and Shun, carnival with the appliers and destroyed with Jie and Zhou, and prosperous with Tang and Wu. If you think the Tao is very close? But it is indeed in the distant four poles; think that the Toa is far away, but it is always by my side; think that the Toa is very dim, but its brilliance is very obvious; think the Toa is very easy, but it is very esoteric. It can create the heaven and the earth, and can resolve the great violent thunder; everything in the universe is generated by it." Only the mind, which is vast and empty can understand the true meaning of the Tao and realize the truth of the Tao.

Ms. Ma Xiaoqiu was born with amazing qualities and she is enlightened by words at once. She is deeply versed in the truth of the "Sutra of Pure and Calm". "The Tao is intangible, creating the heaven and the earth; The Tao operates the sun and the moon without affection; The Tao is nameless, raising all things of the universe." In the universe, from the infinite-Tao to the Extreme-Tai chi, the congenital gods do not move without desire, the acquired physical mortal gods move with desires that must return to the congenital, can be naive and sincere. Zen Taoist studies of the heaven and the human beings, it does not stand apart, not be dirty, not be clean, not increase or decrease, the Toa is all. What is even rarer is that Ms. Ma Xiaoqiu can combine Zen with Confucianism, and it is impressive that she has made the three teachings good for business. Taoism's "Tao is natural", Confucian "the benevolent loves others", Zen's "mind without stagnation", these three realms are reflexive from the mind to the substance, practice, the peace of mind, standing up, living in the world, the mind and the body quiet and clear, all the scenes of things, the wise speculation about the life and the world of the sage of the Chinese culture, is obvious on paper.

"Those who are good at ancient times are subtle and profound."
The so-called profound is the Toa, the mind. The Tao is invisible, and the mind is empty. Ms. Ma Xiaoqiu has a deep insight into her spiritual roots, saying that "the Tao is empty, containing everything, without distinction between the good and the evil". From Taoism to Buddhism, she has a corresponding attitude towards the "Heart Sutra". The *Heart Sutra* is the core of the six hundred volumes of the Prajna. For the wisdom of the Prajna, those who had gone into the depth, knowing its taste, are very few. The *Qiu's Monogati* said: "With or without, the color or the empty, moving or static, bending or straight, the rational person is standing in the middle of the non-dark and unclear way." There are mysterious and mysterious, the door of the wonderful things, the sad and wise double fortunes. How many people can understand the transformation of the environment with mind? The Tao in the middle is very difficult. The *Analects of*

Confucius·Yong says: "The Middle Course is also a virtue, and it is almost." The middle is the right Tao of the world, the true Toa also.

Emptiness gives birth to tens of thousands of laws, that is to say, the mind is born with thousands of methods. Zen seeks for the spiritual feeling. Ten thousands of laws are derived from the origin, and destroyed from the origin too. Generate, live, break, emptiness. The causes are born from the mind. The mind is born with the laws. The mind is destroyed together with laws. When Master Hong Ren said to Hui Neng that "Act on without the color mind", Ancestor Six was enlightened at once and said: What is the nature of self? It is clean! What is the nature of self? It is not born and immortal! What is the nature of self? It is self-sufficient! What is the nature of self? It is unshakable! What is the nature of self? It can create all laws!

Confucianism speaks of the world law, and the most subtle part of the world law is the mind. Wang Yangming, a Master of Confucianism in the Ming Dynasty, came into Buddhism and returned to Confucius and Mencius. He had four sentences known to the world: "It is the body to be no good and no evil. It is an action to be good or evil. It is conscience knowing the good and knowing the evil. It is a study of the truth of things to uphold the good and eliminate the evil." The essence of the mind is the heavenly principle, without a single selfish meaning, like a mirror, without good or evil, without substance. When the mind and matter are connected, the feeling is accomplished; there is an intention of the good and the evil. The mind can know Tao, know the Heaven, can sense and enlighten, can know the good and the evil, can examine and rule. To study the truth of things is to study one's mind. Get rid of the error and make the mind right. The mystery of the mind study is not to be biased, not to be empty, pointing to the mind, directing to the Middle Course.

The most quintessence of Yang Ming's psychology is to regard things with mind. The *Biography* has such a classic record: Mr. Yang went to visit Nan Zhen. A friend pointed to the flowers and trees in the rocks and asked: "There is nothing in the world out of our mind, so the flowers in the mountains open themselves up and down, what does it matter to my mind?" Mr. Yang said: "When you don't look at this flower, this flower is silent as the same as your mind; when you look at the flower, the color of the flower is clear for a while, so you know that the flower is not outside your mind."

The unity of knowledge and action is the truth that mind and object reflect each other. Wang Yangming once made a poem *Chanting Four Poems of the Conscience for the Students*: "Everyone has his own Plate needle, and the root of changes is always in the mind. But he laughs at the way of things before that always turned upside down, and the branches and leaves were found outside." The mind is the source of all kinds of changes. Seek not for the mind, but for the things, not from the inside but from the outside. Leave the mind to seek the origin. Don't you reverse your dream?

In the *Qiu's Monogati*, you can see the enlightening senses everywhere. The way of the enterprise management is complicated and simple. Lay down the ego and achieve the altruism, always in meditation, everywhere cultivation, the mind and the spirit are bright. The enlightening is the light of the mind, which is where human nature stands. Man is the centre of the heaven and earth. It is precisely this that Song Confucians teach people to "set their minds for the world." In the *Biography*, while Master Yang Ming talked with his students and friends on Tao. He said: "What is the center of the heaven and the earth, when you look at them?" The answer: "It is said that man is the center of the heaven and the earth." He asked: "What is the mind of the man?" The answer: "It is just a spirit." The *Qiu's Monogati* holds the mission of "prospering the industry to benefit the people", with the business philosophy "selflessness, altruism, specialization, trustworthiness" that is the spirit feeling up the Heaven and the earth. With this mind, and the root of this spiritual knowledge, the world will live endlessly forever.

Therefore take it as the preface.

Han Wangxi

自　序

"岁月本长，而忙者自促；天地本宽，而鄙者自隘；风花雪月本闲，而扰攘者自冗。"

不少人曾问过我，你的事业版图拓展得这么大，用日理万机来形容也不为过，为何还能坚持用文字的方式来跟大家分享智慧？我想用这个故事回答他们：许多年前，我的中学老师，一位满腹经纶、饱经家国离恨的老人，出于对中华传统文化流失的痛惜，将复兴、传承中华传统文化的种子埋到了我的心里。从那时起，传承中华传统文化便成为我一生的梦想。当时我并未预见到我的梦想会顺应时代发展的需求，与习近平主席提出的中国梦契合在一起。

这些年，无论遇到怎样的挫折、磨难，我都未曾放弃过这个梦想，这好像是我的使命与职责。也许真的是人有善愿，天必佑之，愿力有多大，回报有多大，鼎益丰的发展也是这样的水到渠成、道法自然。从个人管理到公司管理，从个人成长到公司成长，不断学习，从古籍中、从现代电影里甚至登高望远，也有别样的景色和体会……

拨开迷雾见本心，本心就是真道。回首来路，这些年我一直孜孜以求的，除了我的梦想，就是真道与智慧，人生经历越多，越让我对古人的智慧感到惊叹与深深的敬畏，给我定力，面对挑战。佛法与因果，一切真实不虚。

所以，我多么渴望更多的人能认识到这些，勤学、善思、笃行，获得美好和幸福的人生。怀着这样的心愿，笔耕不辍，一有新的感悟，就记录下来与人分享。不知不觉，集结成册。《道德经》有81章，《秋言物语》也刚好有81章，记载我的人生感悟和正道。

春秋日长，岁月更迭。当明白专注的重要，确知自己所需要和必须努力的目标时，青春的年华已经过去。负重前行中，好在有了排除一切杂念和欲望的能力。当进取成了唯一的志向，人生的专注也就有了方向。

我已迈进知天命的岁月，但仍有一颗真挚的赤子之心，不管是对梦想还是对真理的追求。出走半生，归来仍是少年。而此少年与彼少年相比，没有了青春的迷茫与无知，也不沾染世俗的污垢，只有对信仰纯澈而执着的坚守，对世界天地万物与真善美的热爱与感动。

少年无惧岁月长。我的追求将继续，我的感悟将继续，而我的分享也将继续……

鼎益丰集团创造人、总裁
深圳市企业联合会副会长
广东省万明子慈善基金会理事长

PREFACE II

" Time is long, but busy men feel it short. The universe is wide, but the humble feel it narrow between the heaven and the earth. The wind and the flowers, the snow and the moon are originally beautiful and idle, but the worried humans bring troubles on themselves."

Many people have said to me that "your career has expanded so much so that it is not an exaggeration to describe you are dealing with a world of problems every day. Why would you still share your wisdom with others by pen?" I want to use the following to answer them:Many years ago, out of regrets for the loss of Chinese traditional cultures, my middle school teacher, an old man full of wisdom and sorrow over a life of separation of the family and the country, sowed the seeds of reviving and inheriting Chinese traditional culture in me. Since then, carrying on the Chinese traditional culture has become my lifelong dream. At that time, I did not foresee that my dream would in time coincide with the Chinese dream outlined and initiated by Chairman Xi Jinping.

All these years, no matter what kind of setbacks and tribulations I have encountered, I have never given up this dream, which seems to be my mission and responsibility. Perhaps it is true that people have good wishes, and the heaven will bless them. How much will power we have, and how much we will have in return, and the growth of Ding Yi Feng is like irrigation is ready when water comes, a natural course, such as is with the Tao.

Mist is thinning and true intention is revealed, the true intention is the truth. Looking back on the way, I have been diligently striving for these years. Apart from fulfilling my dreams, it is the endeavor in seeking after truth and wisdom. The more life experiences I have, the more I marvel at the wisdom of the ancients with deeper awe. Buddhism and cause and effect are all true.

Therefore, I am eager for more people to recognize this, diligence, good thinking and practice, to obtain a better and happy life. With such a wish I keep pen to paper, and once I have new insights, I record them and share them with others. Unconsciously, it has been able to assemble into a book.

Spring turns into fall, years after year. When understanding the importance of concentration and knowing what's needed to know and the goals that must be reached for, the youthful years have passed. In the process of shouldering weight forward, it is comforting to have possessed the ability to eliminate all distractions and desires. When enlightenment becomes the only ambition, the focus of life has a direction.

I have entered the age of knowing one's destiny, but I still have a heart of youth, be it in pursuing my dream or the pursuit of truth. After half a lifetime outside, returning is still a teenager. Compared to that youth, this youth has no more youthful confusion and ignorance, nor contaminated with secular pollution, only the pure pursuit for faith; affection for the world of heaven and earth, and the love of truth, goodness and beauty.

The youth is not afraid of time, long or short. My pursuit will continue, my sentiment will continue, and my sharing will continue.

Ma Xiaoqiu

目 录 CONTENTS

OI

当下决定未来

The present determines the future

让思想插上翅膀
Thoughts can fly very high

当我们活明白的时候，就不再喜欢那些不切实际的高谈阔论了。因为高谈阔论的时候总要想想自己的行为和当下的言论是否匹配，如果不匹配，我们最好还是不要妄语，妄语有害而无益。思想可以飞得很高，但实际的行为才能决定我们所要去的方向。华丽的辞藻，花拳绣腿般的效仿，距离我们的行为甚远。这样不切实际的语言，永远填不满空虚的世界。

我认为一个人如果不爱祖国不爱党，就跟不爱公司不爱家是一样的。公司是因缘造化、生存和发展、种善或种恶的业力场所。家无论在什么样的状况下，都是我们善恶因缘的落脚点。这四大因缘都是我们自己言行的前因后果。因此今天我们以什么样的方式和态度来对待当下的一切，必将决定我们明天的生存状况。

When we are awake, we no longer like those unrealistic talks. Because when we are talking, we have to think about whether our actions match with what we're saying. If they don't match, we'd better not speak rant. The rant is harmful and useless. Thoughts can fly very high, but actual behavior can determine the direction where we want to go. Gorgeous words and embroidered imitations are far from our behavior. Such an impractical language can never fill up the empty world.

I think that if one does not love his motherland and does not love the party, it is the same as not loving the company and not loving his family. The company is a karmic place of the origin, survival and development, a place of karma for good or evil. No matter what kind of situation the family is in, it is the place where we are bound for good or evil. These four major causes are our own karmas. Therefore, what kind of approach and attitude we use today to treat everything we have today will surely determine our survival tomorrow.

02

知足常乐，一切都是上天最好的安排

Happiness comes from contentment; everything is the
best arrangement in universe

成功的道路是穿越一条条封锁线

The road to success is
through one blockade after another

知足常乐是我们身心修养到一定境界，由内心深处所发出的一种声音。这声音是宁静的，它不会因金钱和地位而泛起丝毫的涟漪。金钱有可能是能力的代表，但同时也是欲望的量化指数，知足是对欲望的无形限制。

夜深人静的时候，和自己的心灵对话是静默中的升华。因为有黑夜，我们才能与精神相伴；因为有黑夜，万物才能得以舒缓。黑夜之所以不与白天同行，是因为它不欲求白天的光明，却独享着黑暗的寂静。

我们每个人年轻的时候都会有这样的经历：做一件事情遭遇挫败的时候，都会反思和后悔，反思着某一个环节的失误或者后悔当初的选择。我们大可不必如此，孰不知失败是通往成功的阶梯，每一次失败都让我们向成功迈进了一步！但有人会在失败时选择退却，也有人会选择坚守，并最终成为胜者。人生的每一段经历对于我们而言都是必然的，也是必要的。

有句歌词这样说，"没有风雨躲得过，没有坎坷不必走"，一切都是上天最好的安排。失败是上苍对我们的恩赐，因为你是可塑之材，老天才以种种方式锤炼你。只有经受住考验，不怕千难万险，才能成功。成功的道路就是穿越一条条封锁线。

T he contentment is a sound that comes from the depth of our mind when our spiritual cultivation is to a certain level. This sound is quiet and it does not fluctuate because of the status of money. Money may be a representative of ability, but it is also a quantitative index of desire. Contentment is an intangible restriction on the desire.

In the dead of night, the dialogue with oneself is the sublimation in silence. Because of the darkness, we can be accompanied by our spirit. Because of the darkness, everything can be relieved. The reason why the darkness does not walk with the daytime is because it does not desire the light of the day, and thus enjoys the silence of the darkness.

When we were young, we would have the experience that when something was done wrong, we would introspect and regret the original choice or a certain link with the failure. In fact, that is not the case. Actually, the failure is the ladder to success. Every failure makes us take a step toward to success! But there are those who choose to retreat after failure and those who succeed to persist. Every experience of life is inevitable and necessary for us.

There is a lyric that sings like "No wind and rain can be escaped, no bumps could be skipped", everything is the best arrangement in heaven. Failure is God's gift to us. Because you are a talented person, God will temper you in various ways. We can succeed only if we stand the tests and are not afraid of difficulties. The road to success is through one blockade after another.

03 ──────────────────

看不见、摸不着，但它有作用
Invisible, intangible, but it works

文字所蕴含的老子智慧，才是最重要的"果实"
The Lao Tzu's wisdom contained in the text
is the most important "fruit"

　　坚持每天诵读《道德经》，真的能带给我们很大的好处。经典是由文字写就的，但字里行间所蕴含的老子的智慧，才是最重要的

"果实"。我们每天读经典，其实就是在学习圣贤的智慧；每一天重复做一件事，你就会从中获得能量。

我们可能看不见能量是怎样到我们身上来的，就像老子在《道德经》中所说，道不可捉持，听不到、看不到，但是它有作用。我们现在用的手机就是如此，我给你打电话的时候，你能看得到音波是怎样传导的吗？看不见、摸不着，对吧？但是你在另一边就能听到我的声音。这就是道，看不到、摸不着，但它有作用。

Adherence to reading the *Tao Te Ching* every day really brings us great benefits. The classics are composed of characters, but the Lao Tzu's wisdom contained in the text is the most important "fruit". We read the classic every day. In fact, we are learning the wisdom of the sages. Do one thing repeatedly every day, and we will gain energy from it.

We may not see how the energy comes to us. Just as Lao Tzu said in the *Tao Te Ching*, the Tao can not be seized, heard or seen, but it does work. This is the case with the mobile phones we use now. When I call you, can you see how the sound waves are conducted? Invisible, intangible, right? But you can hear my voice on the other side. This is Tao, invisible and intangible, but it works.

04

智慧与圆融
Wisdom and harmony

收获美，收获智慧；圆融、慈悲与包容

Harvest beauty, harvest wisdom;
harmony, mercy and tolerance

我发现，不想荒废时间的人无论在什么情况下，都可以有收获。散步、聊天、逛街、看电影、听音乐，甚至"葛优躺"，这些举动但凡是人都曾有过。但我们在这些场景下如何收获呢？心是眼睛的主导，眼睛是思想的工具。只要用心去调动眼睛，用神去察言观色，就能得到一个较高层次的收获。除了眼睛看到的物质世界之外，更有无限广阔的精神世界。所以，不同的人，在同一场景下会有不同的收获。智慧的仓库无穷之大，就看我们怎样去收纳……

　　常言道："酒逢知己千杯少，话不投机半句多。"知己可遇而不可求。与知己的对话，是在同一个思想境界和同一种心灵频谱里面进行的。知己之间一次畅快淋漓的交流，除了语言撞击出来的火花之外，还有语言无法替代的心心相印、心领神会的精神契合。

　　当然，在现实生活中，我们或多或少都要面临很多不同频道的对话。这时的交流，要么是为了达成某种目的的手段，要么纯是消耗时间和精力的废话。

　　能够达到目的的对话过程，其实是一种智慧的表现和修养的流露。这时需要圆融的智慧、慈悲的心肠、善解人意的包容。只有这样，我们才能和光同尘，求同存异，由此达到一个互惠共赢的平衡点。

I have found that the people who do not want to waste time can gain in any situation. Walking, chatting, shopping, watching movies, listening to music, or even "getting good while lying", these actions are most commonly seen by the people. But how do we achieve under these scenarios? The mind is the dominant of the eyes, and the eye is the tool of the thought. As long as we mobilize our eyes with our mind and to look at things with the mind, we will get a higher level of gains. In addition to the material vision seen by the eyes, there is an infinitely broader spiritual world. Therefore, different people will have different gains in the same scenario. The wisdom of the warehouse is endless, it depends on how we want to receive...

As the saying goes, "When drinking with a bosom friend, a thousand cups are too few; while arguing with a friend half a sentence is too long." The Confidant can be met without seeking. The confidant dialogue is conducted within the same ideological realm on the same spiritual spectrum. A lively exchange between confidants, apart from the sparks from the words, there is also a spiritual channel that can't be replaced by the language and the mind is in touch.

Of course, in the real life, we have to face more or less different channels of dialogue. The exchange at this time is either a means to achieve a certain purpose or pure nonsense that consumes time and energy.

The dialogue process that can achieve the goal is actually a manifestation of wisdom and accomplishment of cultivation. At this time, the wisdom of harmony and mercy compassion, understanding tolerance are needed. Only in this way can we achieve a balance of mutual benefit and win-win cooperation.

05 ————————————————

虚空之大与不争之德
Great void and undisputable virtues

日月之行，若出其中。星汉灿烂，若出其里

The sun and moon seem to rise from the universe,
and the splendid galaxy seems to flow within it also

　　孩童时，我曾仰望浩渺星空，无数次想知道天上到底有多少颗星星。当时幼小的心灵，稚嫩的思想，我数了很多次都没有结果，只能深叹星星之繁多，以及人之稀少（年幼的我所见所识的人很少）。我那个年龄甚至不知星星为何物。

　　长大后才明白，宇宙之所以浩瀚，是因为无边无际的虚空容纳了无穷无尽的星体。这些人类用尽所有方法和才智都无可计量的星体，都按照各自的轨道周而复始地运行，有条不紊。"日月之行，若出其中。星汉灿烂，若出其里。"这种无法测度的推动力，源自于虚空的无穷之大和星体之间的不争之德。

　　相较于浩瀚的虚空，人是根植地球的生命体。因缘际会，让我们走在了一起。但太多的迷惑与障碍使我们迷失本性，既不知自己从何而来，更不知自己为何而来。我们在不明不白中活着。故此，

我们很容易被污染，我们的自私和贪婪都来自后天的污染。贪财、贪色、贪爱、贪情，这一切都是争，都是自私的表现。有了贪欲，就有了执着；有了执着，就有了忧愁、烦恼和悲苦；然后随之而来的就是生、老、病、死。

　　然而，虚空之大，永恒之久！星球之多，无可穷尽！它们长久不灭，完美体现了老子在《道德经》揭示的哲理："以其不自生故能长生。"人与之相比，何其渺小！我们要以虚空之大，映照和扩充我们的心量；要以星体的不争之德，澡雪我们的心灵，学会随缘自在，与道相应。

When I was a child, I used to look up at the vast sky. I wondered how many stars are there in the sky? At that time, with my young mind and immature thoughts, I counted stars many times without result. I could only sigh deeply about the variety of stars

and the scarcity of people (there were few people I met and knew). At my age that time I did not even know what were the stars.

When I grew up, I realized that the universe is vast because the infinite void holds the infinite planets... These planets are beyond measure, even if the men use all means and wisdom still in vain. The planets are all operating on their own orbits and in an orderly manner. The sun and moon seem to rise from the universe, and the splendid galaxy seems to flow within it also. This unmeasured impetus stems from the invincibility of the void and the indisputable virtue between the planets.

Compared to the vast void, people fall into the earth's living body. However, too many confusions and obstacles have caused us to lose our nature. We do not know where we came from, nor do we know why we came. We live in uncertainty. Therefore, we are easily contaminated, and our selfishness and greed are all caused by pollution. Desire, lust, love, passion, all need to struggle and all are selfish manifestations. There is greed, there is perseverance. The perseverance certainly leads to sorrow, trouble, and misery, and what follows is the duration of life, aging, sickness, and death.

However, the vast void is long-lasting! The planets are infinite! Their long-lasting immortality perfectly reflects the philosophy revealed by Lao Tzu in the *Tao Te Ching*: "It can live forever without its own sake". How small is man compared to the nature! We must reflect and expand our minds with the vast void; we must bathe our minds with the undisputable virtue of the planets and learn to be ease with the Tao.

治企之道，亦繁亦简

The way to manage enterprises,
complexity and simplicity

无我、利他、专一、守信

Selflessness, altruism,
specialization, trustworthiness

秋言物语

说到企业管理，我认为它既复杂又简单，复杂是简单的过程。

年轻的时候做企业，往往把简单的事情复杂化。人生是一个既漫长又短暂的过程，我们年轻时没有足够的经历和经验，在生活和工作的实际运作中，常会遭遇种种理想与现实的偏差和背离。无论我们多么激情澎湃，也阻挡不住理想的沉沦。我们带着希望迎着朝阳启程，却往往抱着失败伴随着黑暗伤悲。这样的经历叠加了，我们也就成熟了。我们成熟了，也就不再年轻了。人不怕不年轻，就怕不成熟。

所以，经历了、实践了，最后我们才会真的读懂什么叫"大道至简"。大道是方法，至简是过程。

管理企业是一个由复杂到简单的过程，只有经历这样的过程，才能到达至简而无为的境界。这其中皆是领导者的修为。企业领导者，不仅要身先士卒，更要有充分的智慧和缜密的谋划，矢志不移地做到"无我、利他、专一、守信"。这八个字，正是管理企业的良谋和方法。

When it comes to business management, I think it is both complicated and simple, and complexity is in a simple process.

When you're young, doing business often complicates simple things. Life is a long and short process. When we were young, we did not have enough experience. In the actual operation of life

and work, we often encountered deviations and reversion from ideals and realities. No matter how passionate we were, we could not stop the ideal wheel from falling. We set out to meet the rising sun with hopes, but they often held defeats with dark sadness. This experience stacks up and we are mature. When we are mature, we are no longer young. People are not afraid of being young; they are afraid of being immature.

Therefore, through the experience, practice, and finally we will really understand what is called "the truth is simple". The truth is the method, and the simplicity is the process.

Managing a business is a complex to simple process. Only by going through such a process can we reach a state of simplicity. This is all leaders' cultivation. Business leaders must not only take the lead, but also must have sufficient wisdom and good planning. They must do their best to achieve "selflessness, altruism, specialization, trustworthiness". These four characters are good plans and methods for managing enterprises.

善念善行与厚积薄发

Good heart accumulates good deeds;
Save more, release slowly

祸福无门，唯人自招

Misfortunes and happiness are not preordained;
they are created by oneself

　　我们常常看到有人运气很好，好事都被他遇上，而有人却总是走背运，凡事都不顺利。这是什么原因呢？

古圣先贤告诉我们："祸福无门，唯人自招。"这一句话让我们明白了：人生所有的好运和背运，都是我们自己造成的。但是，人都是父母所生，换言之，人都是情欲的产物，也可以说是欲望催生的生命体。故此，我们从落入人间的那一刻起，就面临沾染不良品行的可能，比如自私和贪欲，等等。所以，后天教育就显得尤为重要。

都说父母是孩子的第一位老师，的确如此。父母的言传身教会自觉或不自觉地、潜移默化地影响着孩子的一生。

出生在什么样的家庭，这是我们自身的因缘果报。古圣先贤又告诉我们："积善之家，必有余庆；积恶之家，必有余殃。"足见家庭教育对孩子的成长至关重要！它对孩子将来走好运还是走背运，起着决定性的作用。

好运和善念善行密不可分，背运和恶念恶行紧密相连。好人是不起恶念、不动恶行的人。善念善行者，必承好运！

关于"厚积薄发"在企业管理中的应用，我有两点心得分享给大家。

第一，企业资金的配置决定着企业的生存和发展。用企业资金量的70%~80%作为不动积蓄，用20%~30%的资金进行投资再创新，这就叫"厚积薄发"。

第二，企业领导者和管理者以及全体员工在功德力方面的积蓄，是企业资本积蓄的无形财富。这需要企业领导者以身作则，带领全体员工行善积德，持之以恒，形成厚德，从而"厚德载物"。少私、寡欲，秉德深厚，载育万物，这也叫"厚积薄发"。

We often see some people with good luck; they are often met with good things. But some people are always with bad luck, everything is not going well. What is the reason for it?

The ancient sages told us that "Misfortunes and happiness are not preordained; they are created by oneself." This makes us understand: All the good luck and unfortunate in life are caused by ourselves. However, people are born of their parents. In other words, people are the products of passion, and they can also be said the life of lust. Therefore, from the moment we fall into the human world, we carry many undesirable factors. such as selfishness and greed etc. Therefore, education is particularly important.

It is said that parents are the first teachers of their children. That's true. Both parents will consciously or unconsciously influence the child's life.

What kind of family we are born into? This is our own retribution. The ancient sages and saints told us: "If you do much good, you will get a good return. If you do much evil, you will get a bad return." It can be seen that the family education is crucial for the child's growth! It plays a decisive role in the child's future good luck or bad luck.

Good luck and good deeds are linked, and bad luck is closely linked to the evil thoughts and bad deeds.

Good people have no evil thoughts and acts. Good people have good ideas and good deeds, and certainly have good luck!

With regard to the application of "Save more, release it slowly", that is to say, one lays a solid foundation of virtue for himself, his life will be shining in the future in business management. I have two points to share with everyone.

First, the allocation of corporate funds determines the survival and development of the company. Use 70%~80% of corporate funds as immovable savings, use 20%~30% of funds to re-create investment, which is called "Save more, release it slowly".

Second, the accumulation of corporate leaders, managers and all employees in the merits and virtues is an intangible warehouse for corporate capital savings. This requires the leaders of the company to set a good example to lead all employees to do good deeds and accumulate virtues, persevere, form a collective virtue, so that "Great virtue bears good wealth". "Less private, less desires, deeper virtues, and bearing all things", this is also called "Save more, release it slowly".

爱是前世的因、今生的缘

Love is the cause of the past life,
fate of this life

爱情，也会随着生命而成、住、坏、空

Love is also getting along with the process of generating,
growing, deteriorating and empty

　　就爱情而言，我想，人世间有多少个人，就有多少种爱。没有哪一种爱可以成为人类爱的标准。但我们必须清楚，无论什么样的爱情都不可能长久，这就是人世间这个空间维度的成、住、坏、空。彼此相爱成就一段感情，双方因爱而住在彼此的心里，时间长了开始厌倦，最后导致分离，这就是爱情成、住、坏、空的过程。

　　爱，是前世的因、今生的缘。我们今生无论遇到谁，都是在了缘。所以，无论是相爱，还是相爱之后的分离，都是在了却一段因缘。既然都是了却，那过程只是时间长短不同而已。年轻人幻想爱情天长地久，殊不知即使钟爱一生，爱情也会随着生命而成、住、坏、空。

　　看清爱情的真相，了却一段因缘，经历一段痛苦，收获一种成长，觉悟一种智慧。感谢彼此成就！祝福对方幸福吉祥！

In the terms of love, I think there are as many kinds of loves as there are people in the world. No kind of love can be the standard of human love. However, we must make it clear that no matter what kind of love can't last forever. This is the dimension of space of the human world, the generation, growth, deterioration and vacuum. Love each other to achieve a relationship, the two sides live in each other's mind because of love, a long time began to get bored, and finally lead to separation, which is the process of love, living, bore, apart.

Love is the cause of past lives and the fate of today's life. No matter who we meet in this life, we are in the balance of causes. Therefore, whether in love, or after the separation of love, is in a relationship. Since it is all, the process is only different in length of time. Young people dream about love forever, and they don't know that even if they love for a life, wish to love forever, but it is always getting along with the process of love, living, bore, apart.

To see the truth of love, to end a certain cause, experienced a period of pain, gain a kind of growth, realize a kind of wisdom. Thanks for your mutual growth! Blessing each other auspicious happiness!

从雾霾看阴阳祸福

Through the smog, see clearly:
Yin and Yang, misfortune and blessing

一阴一阳之谓道

Yin and Yang are the truth of
the universe

上周四我乘飞机去了北京。当天下午四点多的时候，飞机平稳着陆。走出机舱，一股柴火燃烧的味道弥漫在空气之中。环顾四周，仰望天空，天色阴沉。蓝天白云被游离在空气中的尘霾遮蔽得严严实实。不禁喟然！首都——北京！

雾霾！这种人类在推动物质文明发展的进程中，由于工业不断扩张而产生的大量污染物，侵占了我们赖以生存的空间。大街上，无数张戴着口罩的脸，无数辆装着空气净化器的汽车。来去匆匆的人们就这样活着⋯⋯

透过此现象，我们再一次明白了人类这个空间维次的阴阳之理。

古语云："一阴一阳之谓道"。阴阳是事物正反、好坏的两个方面。人类物质需求的急剧扩大，迫使我们不断地发明创造出新的事物。人类在享受物质发展带来的各种便利和舒适的同时，也在品尝着物质文明所带来的苦果。

由此可见，人类所有的发明创造，都必然产生两种结果——好的和坏的。这就是事物的两个方面，换言之，也叫阴阳的两个方面。阴与阳，矛与盾，都不是孤立存在的。阴阳互动，矛盾共存，相互牵制，相互促进，从而推动事物的发展变化。

重要的是，我们如何应用阴阳之理，合理有效地把握当下，并创造未来。在此，我不禁想起老子《道德经》中的一句话："祸兮福之所倚，福兮祸之所伏。"祸福不单行啊！

I arrived in Beijing at 4pm last Thursday. Walking off of the plane, there was a burning smell of firewood in the air. I looked around me, trying to determine where the smell was coming from. I looked up at the sky and the sky was dark - what was supposed to be blue sky and white clouds were covered with impurities in the air. I cannot help but lament: this is our capital, Beijing!

Smog! In the process of promoting and developing a material lifestyle, human beings have caused vast pollution, pollution which we now have to live with. On the street, countless faces wear masks and countless cars have air purifiers. People to wrapped up in the hustle and bustle of the city seemed to have normalized living like this.

We have once again understand that humanity is the Yin and Yang principle of this dimensional space.

As the old saying goes, "Yin and Yang are the truth of the universe." Yin and Yang are the two sides of things: the positive and the negative, the good and the bad. The rapid expansion

of the material needs of mankind forces us to constantly invent and innovate and enjoy the convenience and comfort brought about by material development. Little did we realize that in the process of enjoying, we also tasted the bitter fruits brought about by a civilization that emphasis the material civilization.

It can thus be seen that all human inventions and creations will inevitably produce two kinds of results - good and bad. This is the two aspects of all things. In other words, it is also called two aspects of Yin and Yang. Yin and Yang, light and dark, spears and shields do not exist in isolation. Contradictions coexist, mutual containment, mutual promotion, and thus promote the development of things.

What is important is how we apply the principles of Yin and Yang, to understand what is happening around us as a whole rationally and effectively and create a future. Here, I can not help but think of a sentence in Lao Tzu's *Tao Te Ching*: "Blessings and misfortunes come in turn." That is to say, bad things can lead to good result. Good things can lead to bad results. Blessings and misfortunes are travel together.

10

中医与西医之我见
Thoughts on Chinese traditional medicine
and western medicine

人类所有的发明创造都是应运而生
All human inventions
and creations come into being

  说到中医，最近在我身上发生了一件令人惊叹的事：一位中医教授用老祖宗传下来的中医经络穴位调理法，只用了三次六小时，就把我身体各部位多余的脂肪去除了 40%～70%，尤其是背部的脂肪。这种不可思议的神奇效果，让我惊喜之外，更让我深深地思索……

  透过历史的长河，我们发现从春秋战国中医理论基本形成算起，中医的历史已有两千多年。两千多年的沉淀是何等的厚重！但近几十年来，我们把老祖宗留下的大量瑰宝丢失了！凡事皆有因果。

  随着人类社会的高速发展，中医辨证施治、标本兼治的方法已无法满足人类的所有治疗需求。18世纪的工业革命给西方带来了急剧的社会变革，也推动了西医的发展；而第一次、第二次世界大战中对大量伤兵的救治需求，则加速了西医的发展。西医着眼于物质的一面，治疗侧重从物质层面入手。中医则着眼于物质和精神两个

方面，以阴阳理论为基础，辨证施治，以达到标本兼治的目的。

　　或许有人会问："到底是西医好，还是中医好？"我的回答是："两者都好，又都各有不足。"凡事没有绝对的好与坏，人类所有的发明创造都是应运而生，是事物发展变化的必然结果。中医和西医，各有优点，也各有不足，两者应该共生互补。我们既要利用好西医的优势，也要传承好中华两千多年中医的精华，让它们为人类的健康而造福。

S peaking of Chinese traditional medicine, I recently had an amazing thing happening: with the help of a professor of Chinese traditional medicine, who used the traditional Chinese meridian acupuncture conditioning methods passed down by his ancestors, I

managed to expel much of the toxins and excess weight on my body. It took only three or six hours to put off the extra fat in all parts of my body. Nearly 40% to 70% have been removed, especially back fat. This incredible magical effect surprised me and made me think deeply...

Through the long history, we have discovered that since the *Huang Di Nei Jing*, the history of Chinese traditional medicine has been more than 5,000 years. But in recent decades, we have lost a lot of treasure left by our ancestors! There's a reason for everything.

With the rapid development of human society, the treatment of Chinese traditional medicine syndrome differentiation and symptoms and root causes can not meet all human treatment needs. Western industrial revolution in the eighteenth century brought about drastic social changes and promoted the development of western medicine. The large scale trauma and harm caused by the First and Second World Wars created a need to mass and immediate medicine, which accelerated the development of Western Medicine. Western Medicine focuses on the physical side, and treatment focuses on material aspects. Traditional Chinese Medicine focuses on both the physical and spiritual aspects, based on the Yin and Yang theory, and dialectical treatment to achieve the purpose of treating both the symptoms and the root causes.

Some people may ask: "which is better? Western Medicine or Chinese traditional medicine?" My answer is: both are good and they all have their own shortcomings. There is no absolute good or bad in all things, including human inventions and creations. Traditional Chinese Medicine and Western Medicine have their own advantages and disadvantages and as such they should be symbiotic and complementary. We must make good use of the advantages of Western Medicine, and we must inherit the essence of Chinese traditional medicine for more than five thousand years so that they can continue to benefit human health.

汲取道的能量
Absorb the energy from the Tao (Path)

大道无形，生育天地

The Tao is invisible,
created the heaven and the earth

华夏神州，泱泱大国，悠悠五千年的历史文化。五千年，这仅仅是中华文明的史载记录。五千年前呢？地球是什么时候形成的？天地是怎样诞生的？千百年来，人类在不断探索宇宙奥秘的进程中，产生了许多哲学家、历史学家、科学家……

老子，这位天地所造化的圣人，给我们留下了《道德经》。老子仅仅以五千字就揭示了宇宙天地的真理之道："有物混成，先天地生。寂兮寥兮，独立而不改，周行而不殆，可以为天下母。吾不知其名，字之曰道。"这个在天地生成之前就存在的、古往今来独立而永不改变的、周而复始地运行着的混成之物是什么呢？它就是道。道无形无象、无色无味、手摸不着、眼看不见。这种似乎不存在的东西，却有着无穷无尽、不可超越的能量。

《清净经》借老子之口进一步阐述了道的作用："大道无形，生育天地；大道无情，运行日月；大道无名，长养万物。"由此我们明白了道的含义：无形的道可以生育天地，无情的道可以推动日月运行，无名的道可以滋养万物的生长。这种强大而不可战胜的力量就是道的作用。

人可以通过学习和实践来感悟道的存在，并由此获得道的能量：

"大道无形，生育天地"，道之所以具有生育天地的能量，是因为道无形无象，像虚空一样，能容纳万事万物。人要想具备成功的本领，就要做到无我、利他，才能成就一切美好的愿望。

"大道无情，运行日月"，道能够推动日月的运行，是因为道本无情。这里的无情是一种无情胜有情的境界，也就是让我们不要执着于个人的情爱，如亲情、友情和爱情。个人的任何情爱都是小我，把爱放大，爱天下所有人，才能拥有大天下的格局。

"大道无名，长养万物"，道本身是没有名也不求名的，老子想要我们明白真理，所以勉强地为之取了一个"道"字为名。

由此可见，人想要成就一番事业，就要淡泊名利、不求名利，才能获得如同道一般的能量！我赞同一位成功人士所言："大成品质源于厚德，辉煌格局不离大道。"

The Chinese nation, a great country, has a five thousand old history. This five thousand years is just a record of the history of the descendants of Yellow Emperor. What about before those five thousand years? When the earth came into being? How was the world born? For thousands of years, during the process of human exploration of the mysteries of the universe, many philosophers, historians, and scientists have sought to answer this question.

Lao Tzu, a sage created by the heaven and the earth, left us with the Book of Morals, the *Tao Te Ching* . Lao Tzu revealed the truth of the universe with just five thousand words, "There was something that existed before the heaven and the earth. Loneliness and stagnation; it can be the mother of the whole world. I don't know its name, just named 'Tao' . This existed before the heaven and the earth. What is the hybrid that runs before and after the generation of the heaven and the earth; which has been working independently forever and ever since then?" What is the hybrid that operates on a regular basis? It is the Tao. Tao is intangible, colorless and tasteless, untouchable with hands, invisible with eyes. It is seemingly a nonexistent thing, but it has infinite, unsurpassed energy.

The *Sutra of Pure and Calm* further elaborated the role of Tao by Lao Tzu: "The Tao is intangible, creating the heaven and the earth. The Tao operates the sun and the moon without affection. The Tao is nameless, cultivating all things of the universe." From this we understand the meaning of Tao: the invisible Tao can create the heaven and the earth. The merciless Tao can promote the operation of the sun and the moon. The nameless Tao can nourish the growth of all things. This powerful and invincible power is the function of the Tao.

People can realize the existence of Tao through learning and practice, and gain the energy from the Tao.

"The Tao is invisible and created the heaven and the earth." The reason why the Tao has such an energy accomplish this feat is because the Tao is without self and it can accommodate everything. If the people want to have the skills to succeed, they will have to achieve selflessness and altruism so that they can achieve all good wishes.

"The Tao operates the sun and the moon without affection." The Tao can promote the operation of the sun and the moon, because the Tao is ruthless. The ruthlessness here is a state of both detachment and love, that is, let us not cling to personal love, such as affection and friendship., but we must enlarge our love: to love everyone in the world.

"The Tao is nameless, creating all things of the universe." The Tao itself has no name or for name, and Lao Tzu wants us to understand the truth. Therefore, he reluctantly named it "Tao".

From this, it can be seen that if one wants to accomplish something, one must be indifferent to fame and fortune, not seeking fame and fortune to gain the same energy as the Tao! I like the same successful person to say, "Good quality from great morality, and splendid pattern is on the Tao."

12

禅与人生快乐的境界
The realm of Zen and Happiness

专注、专一；情深不寿
Concentration and focus;
feeling too deep leads to a life that can not be long

说到"禅"，绝大部分人一定会想到佛学、佛家。其实，"禅"不是佛家的专利。禅在人们的生活和工作中无处不在。比如，人在科学研究发明、文学艺术创作、企业管理和营运策划，乃至阅读、看电影电视等活动中，都可以不知不觉地完成一次"禅定"的过程。

　　"禅"或者"禅定"，又叫思维修，也就是意念的专一和专注。

　　不同的人有不同的禅境，禅的境界因人而异。老子一生的"禅定"留下了千古不朽的《道德经》五千言。当代乔布斯通过"禅定"创造了众人追逐的"苹果"，阿里巴巴、腾讯无一不是马云、马化腾的"禅定"之作。

　　任何形式的意念专一和专注，都可以称之为"禅"。专心专注、一心一意，时间越长，其定力越大；定力越大，其成就越大。

　　说到"情深不寿"，人们可能难以理解。"情深不寿"的意思是，太执着于情的人寿命不长，这里的"情深"是指对亲情、爱情和友情用情过重。

　　透过文学或现实的人物，我们可以看到很多才情女子命不长，红颜而命薄。《红楼梦》的林黛玉以及饰演林黛玉的陈晓旭、歌手邓丽君、作家三毛等等，她们无一不是情意深重而早离人世的女子。

　　情执尤以女人为重，女人又以爱情为重。一个执着于个人情感的人，其内心深处一定是自私和狭隘的。把情感倾注在某一人身上而不肯放手，天长日久由情生爱、由爱生痴、由痴生苦、由苦生恨、由恨而伤身。由此，健康随着泪水流失，生命在嗔念中缩水。

好男儿志在天下，好女人慈悲喜舍，效法天地无情大爱。这才是人生无比快乐的精神境界。

Speaking of "Zen", most people will certainly think of Buddhism and Buddhists. In fact, "Zen" is not a Buddhist concept. Zen is ubiquitous in people's lives and work. For example, people can meditate without complete understanding of the process of "meditation". Just as people may fall into the realm of Zen in scientific research and inventions, literary and artistic creation, corporate management and operation planning, and even reading and watching movies and television.

"Zen" or "meditation" is also called spiritual cultivation, which is the specificity and concentration of ideas.

Different people have different Zen environments. The realm of Zen varies from person to person. The "meditation" of Lao Tzu left behind the eternal Five Thousand Words of the *Tao Te Ching*. The contemporary Jobs created the "Apple" through "meditation" chased by the mass. Alibaba and Tencent are both Ma Yun and Ma Huateng's creation through "meditation".

Any form of mindfulness and focus can be called Zen. The longer it takes to focus and concentrate, the greater its determination; the greater the determination, the greater its achievement.

There is a phrase "feeling too deep leads to a life that can not be long." Many people may find it difficult to understand.

The "feelings" here refer to over-reliance on affection, love and friendship. So in essence, the phrase means people who are too dedicated to emotions do not have a long life.

Through literary or realistic figures, we can see that many talented women suffer a fate of a short life span. Lin Daiyu from *A Dream of Red Mansions*, Chen Xiaoxu who plays Lin Daiyu, the singer Tang Lijun, and the author San Mao are all deeply emotional, all suffer a tragic fate.

The women are especially all deeply emotional, and women are particularly for love. A person who is attached to personal emotions must be selfish and narrow-minded. Focusing on an individual's emotions and reluctantly letting go: love will make you crazy, suffer by bitterness, hate and bitter, and do harm to your health. As a result, health diminishes with tears and life shrinks in the hatred.

A good man's aspiration is in the world, and a good woman is merciful and joyful, imitating the heaven and the earth. This is the very spiritual realm of life.

13

执古之道，获圆满智慧

Execute the ancient ways to
achieve great wisdom

一阴一阳之谓道

Yin and Yang are
the truth of the universe

今天看到一则报道说：人体的经络，通过科学的方法可以完整地展现了。

"古之善为道者，微妙玄通，深不可识。"《黄帝内经》早在两千多年前就已经确立了经络学说，国人却又再绕了两千多年的大圈后才将之证明，两千多年！仅仅证明了老祖宗的一个命题是正确的。由此，我们不得不思索一个问题：今天的人们，为什么对于许多古代文明所留下的优秀而真实有效的历史文化不加以研究和利用呢？甚至是一味地丢弃呢？其原因在于人们对于自身缺乏相应的认知。例如，我们懂得为我们使用的任何家电产品编写一本说明书，以指导我们正确使用，但是我们不明白人体自身应该如何合理化地使用。《黄帝内经》就是一部人体最为详细的说明书，但我们平常人读不懂，也根本不想读懂，因为奇经八脉我们看不见、摸不着。这就是我们的偏执和我见造成的千古遗憾。

其实究其根本，人类生存在一个物质和非物质的世界，而我们大部分人却偏偏不去发现和研究非物质的存在。老祖宗早就告诉我们一阴一阳之谓道，把握古代之道，懂得阴阳之理，方能获得圆满智慧。

Today I read a report saying: The human body's meridians can be fully seen through scientific methods.

"The ancient virtue is the Tao, subtle, mysterious, deeply indiscernible." *Huang Di Nei Jing* as early as 5,000 years ago has established the theory of meridians. This proves our ancestors' thought process is correct. From this, we have to think about a problem: why do humans today not study the outstanding historical treasures that have been left behind by many ancient civilizations? Even blindly discard it? The reason is that humans lack a lot of awareness about themselves. For example, we know how to write a manual for any household electrical appliances we use to guide us to use them correctly because they offer use immediate and tangible results. However we do not understand how the human body should be used because it is internal. *Huang Di Nei Jing* is the most detailed manual of the human body, but we do not understand it, and we do not want to read it at all, because we cannot see or feel the meridians. This is the eternal regret of our age caused by paranoia and own opinion.

As a matter of fact, human beings live in a material and immaterial world, and most of us do not find and study immaterial existence. The old ancestors long ago told us that one Yin and one Yang are the truth of the universe. Only by learning the ancient saying and understanding the principles of Yin and Yang, can we achieve a perfect wisdom.

I4

知行合一，以天地为榜样

Combining knowledge and practice,
Taking heaven and earth as a model

天地所以能长且久者，以其不自生，故能长生

The world is vast and everlasting,
and it can live forever because it is not selfish

昨晚一段真实的经历让我自省和醒悟：鼎益丰2017迎新年会即将到来，我抽空做了发型。由于我过度地强调头发的卷度，使发型师的注意力集中在头发的卷度而忽略了长度。

头发做完之后，卷度令我满意，但缺憾的是长度不够，短了一点。想到年会的服装和发型有点不匹配，于是怨、恨、恼、怒、烦情不自禁生出，我拿起电话把发型师批评了一顿。十多分钟之后，我感觉到自己的行为不对，一时的怨气不正是自己执着于形象而产生的吗？执着生怨，怨生气，气生怒，我不由得想到了发型师此刻的感受！我心里非常难过，又拿起电话告诉发型师，有补救的办法，可以接长，以此消除发型师的不快和愧疚。今早起床后，我再次打电话跟发型师说了声对不起！

修行无处不在，修行二字也不是宗教的专利。所谓修行就是学

习和实践，学习和实践的不断结合就是知行合一的境界。

人的欲望从五个方面产生：物质财富、男女情欲、地位名利、饮食享受、睡眠之欲。

这五种欲望都是人的本能。是的，没错，我们正是带着五欲而落入人间的俗人。俗人有着俗人境界的聪明才智，但是，俗人的聪明才智都是随着以上五种欲望而产生的，都是利己的。凡是利己的，都是不长久的。圣人老子在《道德经》中讲道："天地所以能长且久者，以其不自生，故能长生。"老子明确地告诉我们：天地之所以长久地存在而不消亡，是因为天地无欲，无欲则无私。

人的财、色、名、食、睡，正好对应着生、老、病、死、苦。我们全可以效仿天地，以天地为榜样，除却五欲，天长地久。

A real experience just last night made me introspective: Ding Yi Feng '2017 annual meeting is coming. I took the time to make a hairstyle. Because I over-stretched on the curls of the hair, the stylist's attention was focused on the curls of the hair and the length of the hair was ignored.

After the hair was finished, the curls of the hair was satisfied to me, but the length was too short. Thinking that the costumes and hairstyle for such an important annual meeting were off, I became consumed with negative emotions such as resentment, hatred, anger, and annoyance. I picked up the phone and criticized the hair stylist. After more than ten minutes, I felt my behavior was wrong. Isn't the momentary grievance caused by my own attachment to my own image? Persistent grudges, resentful anger, I could not

help but think of hair stylist's feelings at the moment. I was very sad in my heart. I picked up the phone again and told the hair stylist I will find a solution to this hairstyle mishap. After getting up this morning, I called the hair stylist again and said I'm sorry!

Examples are everywhere and not just in China. The so-called practice is learning and practice. The constant combination of study and practice is the realm of combining knowledge with practice.

Human desires arise from five aspects: Material wealth; Sexual lust; Status and fame; Enjoyment of food; Desire to sleep.

These five desires are human instincts. Yes, we are the vulgar people who fall into the world with five base desires. But we are also intelligence. The five base desires lead to selfishness. But selfishness is only temporal. The sage Lao Tzu said in the *Tao Te Ching* that "the world is vast and everlasting, and it can live forever because it is not selfish." Laozi told us clearly the reason why the heaven and the earth exist for so long is because heaven and the earth have no desire.

People's wealth, sexuality, fame, food, and sleep correspond to birth, aging, illness, death, and suffering. We can imitate the heaven and the earth, follow the example of the heaven and the earth and put aside the five desires, forever.

I5 ———————————————————

智慧是生存的境界
Wisdom is the realm of survival

智慧是修行的结果

Wisdom is the result of
spiritual practice

这几天，我在和家人、朋友的聚会中，听到这样的话："六年的时间，你把公司做到这么大，并且越做越好，这对我来说简直是个谜。"在此，我想解谜，就从聪明和智慧说起。

通常人们审视一个人或判断一件事物的真假、好坏、对错、高低等等，都是通过眼睛所见、耳朵所听、鼻子所闻、舌头所尝、身体所触、意识所感。殊不知我们的这些感知常常会有差错，差错源于我们有一颗染浊的心。我们有贪心、嗔恨心、愚痴心、邪心、傲慢心。这五种心性是我们智慧的障碍，五心不除，我们永远突破不了聪明的屏障，也就无法达到进入智慧的境界。

人的聪明程度差别不大，但智慧层次有所不同，智慧是修行的结果。知识越多越明智，文化越深越聪慧。聪明是生存的能力，智慧是生存的境界。不吃亏是聪明，吃亏是智慧。聪明追求利益最大化，而智慧者有时赔钱也做得心安理得。

Over the past few days, I have overheard such sentiments at a party with my family and friends: "in six years, you have made the company expend so big, and it's still growing. This is a mystery to me." So, I want to solve this mystery for them. To solve this mystery, I have to start with cleverness and wisdom.

People like to judge a thing's trueness or falseness, goodness or bad, right or wrong, high or low, and so on, usually through the eyes, the ears, the nose, the tongue, the touch, and the sense of consciousness. As everyone knows, these perceptions of ours are often mistakes. The errors stem from the fact that we have an unenlightened mind. We have greed, hatred, ignorance, evil, and

arrogance. These five kinds of minds are obstacles to our wisdom. If we cannot move past these five mindsets, we can never break through and enter the realm of wisdom.

There is little difference in people's potential for intelligence, but the level of intelligence is different. Wisdom is the result of spiritual practice. The more knowledge, the smarter, the more cultural the wiser. Cleverness is the ability to survive, and wisdom is the realm of survival, not suffer from losing is smart and suffering from losing is wisdom. The smart pursuit of the maximization of the benefits, while the wisdom of the people sometimes lose money is also made peace of mind.

16 ——————————————————

以不变应万变
The state of non-change to deal with change

对非对，错非错，凡事皆太极
Right is not right,
wrong is not wrong, all things are too extreme

奔跑的车辆，排放着不计其数的尾气，遮天蔽日。发达的交通，匆忙的脚步，见证着人类在奔跑中不断创造，不断失去。

这些天在台湾考察，从台中到台北，抬头不见蓝天白云，平视则无数车辆前拥后堵。曾几何时，我们头顶着蓝天白云，在清新自然的空气中畅快地呼吸，而今这种欢快的场景逐渐成为一种奢望。这种生态环境的得与失，我们很难断定对与错。对非对，错非错，凡事皆太极。

我们生存的环境变化无常，常人之心亦是如此。但从台中去台北的途中，我们却经历了一次"以不变应万变"的人和事。

从台中到台北两个小时的车程，我们乘坐一辆出租车，司机师傅是一位五十岁左右的男士。我们刚刚坐进车里，他就非常有礼貌地告诉我们：有什么需要可随时向我提出。当时，他这种谦卑的态度就让我感动，觉得他确实就是在全心全意地为我们服务。

走到近一半的路程，司机用非常歉意的口气跟我们说："对不起，我在这里出去一下，耽误几分钟。"我们回应："好的。"结果司机把车很有序地停在车位上，以飞快的速度跑去洗手间，而后又以飞快的速度跑回车里，还不停地说："对不起，不好意思……"

其实我们真的不赶时间，但这位司机师傅一路的态度和表现，让我感受到一种真切的谦卑、诚恳。这种谦卑、诚恳，恰是我们在面对变化无常的人生场景和不同人心时，在一种文化教养之下所呈现出来的以不变应万变的人格品质。

Vehicles emits countless pollutants that scatter in the air. The more cars we have, the faster we move on the roads, they more harm we bring to ourselves.

In Taiwan these days, from Taizhong to Taipei, we can no longer see the blue sky and white clouds. Once upon a time, we had blue sky and white clouds above our heads, breathing in the fresh and natural air. Now this kind of cheerful scene has become a thing of the past. With this kind of ecological environment, we can hardly judge right or wrong. Right is not right; wrong is not wrong. All things are too extreme.

The environment in which we live is fickle and so is ordinary people. However, on the way from Taizhong to Taipei, we have experienced people and things that "No change to deal with change."

We took a two-hour taxi ride from Taizhong to Taipei. The driver was a man about 50 years old. We just got into the car and he told us we could ask him anything at that time. His humble attitude touched me and I felt that he really was trying to serving us wholeheartedly.

Nearly the half way point, the driver told us with a very apologetically, "I'm sorry, I need to pull ver for a few minutes." We responded, "OK." The driver stopped the car at a service area and he dashed to the bathroom. He returned equally hastily, all the while continuing to apologize.

In fact, we really do not have a hurry, but the driver's attitude and performance of the way forward made me feel a real humility and sincerity. This kind of humility and sincerity is precisely the quality of personality that we have shown in the face of changing life scenarios and different people's minds under a culture of cultivation.

I7

过年的愿望与心想事成
New Year's wishes and wishes come true

道成而心想事成
Tao achievement makes
all wishes come true

此刻，窗外一簇浅紫色的小花，在微风中轻轻地摇曳，那轻柔的舞姿，勾起我一段绵柔的回忆……

儿时盼过年，有如饥似渴的感觉。一年对于那个年龄的感觉是那么的漫长！盼望啊！期待！掰着手指头数着新年的到来。

终于过年了！可以从头到脚穿一身新衣！可以随意吃家里任何食物！可以三天不做任何家务！真真切切的欢喜无与伦比！

如今，这些逝去的童年，回不来的欢乐，是岁月沧桑，白了黑发，去了红颜。过年的心愿不为吃穿，只为团圆。

按照中国的民间习俗，初一、十五都会有很多人选择去寺庙或

者宫观烧香拜佛拜道。千百年来这种习俗已深植于中华传统文化的土壤根深蒂固。

春节期间，当我们走进寺庙和道观的时候，会看到烟气缭绕，香火旺盛，芸芸众生，皆有所求。

在佛家的寺庙里我们可以看见"佛法无边"四个大字，在道家的宫观里我们可以看见"道法自然"四个大字。然而我们又对这两句话八个字怎样理解呢？

先说"佛法无边"。就其字意理解，可以解释为佛的方法可以大到无边无际，亦可成就万事万物。但有人会纳闷，我们向佛求了那么多，却成就不了，为什么拜佛不灵呢？简而言之，不灵是因为我们的贪欲大过了本事和德行。只有我们做一个善良慈悲、宽宏大量、乐善好施的人，真真实实地达到"无我、利他、专一、守信"这样一个知行合一的境界，才能在菩萨面前有求必应，这时方能感受到佛法无边无际的能量。

再说"道法自然"。道法是以修道的方法产生的自然能量所成就的事物结果，而非寻常人所思所想的方法。寻常人的方法是阶段性的生灭法，不长久法。因此，由于智慧没有达到一定的高度，就无法洞察未来。不能洞察未来的想法和做法都不叫道法。道法是经过长期不间断修行所成就的法。这其中包括苦行和经历种种磨难，没有经历过生死磨难的人也很难修成道法。道法是成就万事万物的根本方法。道成而心想事成。

At the moment a cluster of light purple swaging gently in the breeze outside the window, that gentle dance, brought me a soft memory……

When I was young I would always be looking forward to New Years. I felt like I was always hungry for the future, counting down towards the new year on your fingertips.

Then, finally, the Chinese New Year comes! You can wear a new clothes from head to toe! Feel free to eat all types of food at home! Can opt out of doing any housework for three days! It's a really happy time.

Looking back, the joys and happiness that come with the New Year are not for food and clothing but for reunion.

According to Chinese folk customs, many people on the first and fifteenth day of the lunar calendar will choose temples or palaces to burn incense and worship Buddhas and Tao. For thousands of years, this custom has been rooted in the soil of Chinese traditional culture and is deeply entrenched.

During the Spring Festival, when we walked into the Buddhist and Taoist temples, we would see smoke lingering, incense burning and all our fellow man each seeking something.

In the Buddhist temple, we can see the phrase "Dharma is boundless." In the Taoist temple, we can see the phrase "Tao is the Nature." However, how do we understand these two phrases?

Let me first talk about "Dharma is boundless." In terms of understanding its meaning, it can be explained that the Dharma can be infinitely large, and that everything can be accomplished. But some people will wonder if we have asked so many about Dharma, but we can't do it. Why should we not achieve from worship Buddhas? In short, it is because our greed is greater than our ability and virtue. Only if we are a kind, compassionate, generous, and charitable will we become a person who truly realizes the state of "Selflessness, altruism, specialization, and trustworthiness". Only in such a state of unity of knowledge and action can we feel the boundless energy.

Then, "Tao is the Nature." Taoism is a method of practicing the Tao, and the result of the natural energy created by it is not what you may think think. The ordinary person's method is a phased birth and death method, not a long-term method. Therefore, because wisdom does not reach a certain height, it cannot be measured in the future. Nothing can be called for without deciding what the future thoughts and practices are. Taoism is a law that has been accomplished through long-term uninterrupted practice. This includes asceticism and all kinds of hardships. Those who have not experienced life or death are also hard to practice Tao. Taoism is the fundamental way to achieve everything. Tao achievement makes all wishes come true.

18

精神文明与物质文明
New Year's wishes and wishes come true

自强不息，厚德载物
Self-improvement
and virtue carry things

如果说企业是圆的，那构成这个圆的一半是文化，一半是经济。文化是精神文明，而经济则是物质文明。

在鼎益丰，人们之所以能获得精神和物质两个方面的收获，关键在于我们一手抓文化，一手抓经济。换言之，我们一手抓精神文明，一手抓物质文明。六年来，我们赢得了成千上万人的拥护和爱戴。

精神文明是整个东方文化的精髓所在，它解决人的意识、伦理、道德、幸福指数以及价值取向等问题。

儒学作为中国本土文化之一，始终强调修身尚德，不鼓励暴力征服。道家更是提倡修养身心，把人和自然看成是有机结合的整体，

从而达到人与自然的和谐相处。同样源于远古文明的中医学从根本上就不提倡对抗性的敌对关系，而讲究相互间的协调与平衡（这一点也是企业管理的关键所在）。基于这样的文明，中华民族从不对外侵略扩张。我们从不把中华优秀的文化转化为向外掠夺的手段。同样，鼎益丰在发展进程中遭到了一些人的诽谤和诋毁，但我们从不以同样的行为去对待诽谤和诋毁我们的人。

说到物质文明，顾名思义，它应该是占有的物质财富在生活和工作中所呈现的各种便利和享受，如舒适美观的办公环境、豪车、豪宅、奢侈品等等。

从某种意义上讲，物质文明也是人类社会发展进步以及人类幸福指数的体现。但我在此所讲的物质文明一定是建立在精神文明之上的，它一定不能脱离"君子爱财，取之有道"，一定不能脱离"自强不息，厚德载物"。

因此，建立一个精神文明和物质文明的共同体，才是企业健康成长和稳步发展的根本所在。

If you say that the company is a round circle, then half of the circle is culture, and the other half is economy. Culture is spiritual civilization, while economy is material civilization.

In Ding Yifeng, the key to people's gaining both spiritual and material wealth is that we have one hand to grasp culture and the other to focus on economy. In other words, we have one hand for spiritual existence and one for material existence. In the past six years we have won the support and love of thousands of people.

Spiritual existence is the quintessence of the entire oriental culture. It addresses issues such as people's consciousness, ethics, morality, happiness, and value orientation.

As one of the Chinese traditional cultures, Confucianism always emphasizes self-cultivation and does not encourage violent conquest. Taoism advocates self-cultivation and regards man and nature as an organically integrated whole so as to achieve harmony between man and nature. Chinese traditional medicine, which also originated from ancient civilizations, does not fundamentally advocate adversarial hostile relations, but emphasizes the coordination and balance between each other (this is also the key to corporate management). Based on this kind of civilization, the Chinese nation never invades and expands externally. We never convert Chinese fine culture into a means of plundering others. In the same way, Ding Yifeng has led to some vilification and denigration. But we never treat our slanders and detractors in the same way.

When it comes to material existence, as its name implies, it's the convenience and enjoyment that material possessions bring to us, such as comfortable and beautiful office environment, luxury cars, luxury houses, luxury goods, and so on.

In a sense, material civilization is also a manifestation of human social development and progress and the human happiness. However, the material existence I am talking about here must be based on spiritual existence. It must not be separated from the "Gentlemen love fortune, in a proper way", and it must not be separated from "Self-improvement and virtue carry things."

For this reason, the establishment of a community of spiritual civilization and material civilization is fundamental to the healthy growth and steady development of the company.

19

读《道德经》有悟
Reading and understanding *Tao Te Ching*

道法自然

Tao comes
from the nature

每天读《道德经》，真有越读越开窍的感觉。《道德经》共八十一章，前三十七章阐述道的本意，后四十四章阐述德的实际效用。故《道德经》的核心就是"道法自然"，整个八十一章都围绕着自然来阐述道和德的意义和作用。

《道德经》是道家思想的代表作。说到道家，人们自然会联想到宗教，当今世界盛行的有佛教、道教、儒教、伊斯兰教和基督教。其实，在我看来五大宗教都是人类智慧的结晶，所谓宗教就是一种文化和文明的传承。佛教以释迦牟尼为代表，道教以老子为代表，儒教以孔子为代表，伊斯兰教以穆罕默德为代表，基督教以耶稣为代表。

以释迦牟尼为代表的佛教告诉人们：要修成正果，其实质就是肉体生命的结束，灵魂生命的再生。以穆罕默德为代表的伊斯兰教告诉人们：慈爱的人死了会去到真主那里。以耶稣为代表的基督教告诉人们：博爱的人死了会升入天堂。以孔子为代表的儒教告诉人们：人要修仁、义、礼、智、信五种品德。

唯有道教偏偏相反，它不研究死的问题，而是致力于研究如何不死的问题。这一思想在《道德经》中随处可见：

"无，名天地之始；有，名万物之母。""天地所以能长且久者，以其不自生，故能长生。""重积德则无不克；无不克，则莫知其极；莫知其极，可以有国；有国之母，可以长久。是谓深根固柢，长生久视之道。"无一不是告诉人们长生久视的方法。

　　天地可以长久。效法天地，国家可以长久，企业可以长久，人当然也可以长久。因此，《道德经》是一本教人明白自然之道乃永久生存之道的教科书。

If you read the *Tao Te Ching* every day, you will have a feeling of understanding more and more and you will obtain a sense of enlightenment. The *Tao Te Ching* has 81 chapters. The first 37 chapters describe the original meaning of the Tao, and the latter 44 chapters describe the actual utility of virtue. Therefore, the core of the *Tao Te Ching* is "Tao comes from the nature". The entire 81 chapters are close to the nature to explain the meaning and the role of Taoism and morality.

The *Tao Te Ching* is a masterpiece of Taoist thinking. When it comes to Taoism, people naturally think of religion. Today's world is a wealth of different religions and beliefs: Buddhism, Taoism, Confucianism, Islam, and Christianity. In fact, in my opinion, the five major religions are the crystallization of human wisdom. The so-called religion is the inheritance of a culture and civilization. Buddhism is represented by Sakyamuni, Taoism is represented by Laozi, Confucianism is represented by Confucius, Islam is represented by Muhammad, and Christianity is represented by Jesus.

Buddhism represented by Buddha Shakyamuni tells people: To achieve a positive result, the essence is the end of physical life and the regeneration of soul life. Islam, represented by Muhammad, tells people: If a loving person dies, he will go to Allah. Christianity, represented by Jesus, tells people of forgiveness and Heaven. Confucianism, represented by Confucius, tells people that people must cultivate five types of virtues: benevolence, righteousness, courtesy, wisdom, and faith.

Only Taoism, on the contrary, does not study the problem of death, but studies on how to prolong the life. This idea can be seen everywhere in the *Tao Te Ching*: "No name" is the beginning of the heaven and the earth; "the names" are born of all things. "The heaven and the earth are so grand and eternal that they can live forever because they are not self-born." "Deep virtue is not competent, without competence, the ability is unlimited, and the ability is unlimited enough to maintain the country. The foundation of the state can be preserved for a long time." Both are telling people the method how to live long with broad vision.

The world can be long. If we follow the example of the heaven and the earth, the country can be long-term, the company can exist and flourish for a long time, and people can also stay for a long time. Therefore, the *Tao Te Ching* is a textbook of the way of the nature to live forever that teaches people how to understand the truth of the nature.

取天下常以无事
Govern the country with the principle of
not intimidating the people as the rule

为学日益
Learn more and
increase more daily

　　人生就是一个不断学习和提升的过程，从小学到高中，从高中到大学，我们完成一个又一个学业，知识随着我们的学业不断增加，我们的大脑填满了各种知识，老子称之为："为学日益。"

　　人生可以有另一种因缘，那就是证道，证道就是用道的方法来生活和工作。这时我们就要渐渐忘却过去由学业带给我们的各种知识，从而进入一个道的境界。当我们的意识不再依赖过去所学的任何知识的时候，才能到达一个无为而无所不为的境界。正如禅易投资法，它的精准度来自完全放空的无为境界，为此老子又称之为："为道日损，损之又损，以至于无为。"

　　当我们忘记所有不利证道的思维和行为的时候，正如鼎益丰的

晨会，读经、听讲，我们从不绞尽脑汁去设计商业模式和管理模式，自上而下，顺应自然。看似天天晨会半天，午休两小时，但六年下来成绩斐然。因此，老子则称之为："取天下常以无事，及其有事，不足以取天下。"

L ife is a process of continuous learning and improvement. From primary school to high school, from high school to university, we have completed one academic study after another. Knowledge increases as our academics continue to increase. As Lao Tzu said, "Learn more and increase more daily."

There can be another kind of relationship in life; that is, to lie by the truth. That is the method of using Tao to live and work. At this time, we will gradually forget about the various kinds of knowledge that have been brought to us by our studies so that we can enter a realm of Taoism. When our consciousness no longer depends on any knowledge we have learned in the past, we can reach a state of inaction and action. Just like the Zen & I-Ching Investment Law, its accuracy comes from the completely empty state of inaction. To this, Lao Tzu also calls it, "To Tao shortcomings decreasing daily, decrease and decrease. Finally, all according to the law."

When we forget all the thoughts and behaviors of unfavorable sermons, just like the Ding Yifeng Morning Reading, and listening, we never brains to design business models and management models, from the top to the bottom, conforming to the nature. Looks like it will be half a day every morning, lunch break for two hours, but six years have made great achievements. Therefore, Lao Tzu once again said, "People who govern the country must often use the principle of not harassing the people as a rule of the country, otherwise it is not worthy of governance."

21 ————————————

无我与专一
No ego but specialization

无我、利他、专一、守信
selflessness, altruism,
specialization, trustworthiness

　　说到"无我"，首先我们要认清"无我"的概念。无是没有，是不存在，是虚无。我是有，是存在，是真实。一个人要真正做到利他，其思想和行为必须上升到无我的境界。这时的"我"，身体是存在的，但心灵是无私的，是完全放下自身所拥有的利益并全心全意为他人而生存。这是一个般若的智慧境界："空不异色，色不异空。"

　　无我是空，全心全意为他人是有，故"有之以为利，无之以为用"。有是我们的身体，身体承载着一颗无私的心，这颗心是胸怀天下的，只有胸怀天下，才能有大用，正如老子所说："圣人无常心，以百姓心为心"，从而天下百姓成就了圣人的地位，这才是一种真正利他的行为。

正如鼎益丰的发展壮大，是因为我们承诺无我，兑现无我，把更多的利益和智慧无私地奉献给大家，大家才成就了鼎益丰的伟大。

　　再言"专一"，专即是一，所谓专一，是一心一意，专心专注在一件事、一个人，或者一个领域等等。专一是心灵清净，思维专注到极致，佛学称之为禅，老子称之为"致虚极，守静笃"。只有这样清净而专注的定力，才能成就非凡的事业，专一可以让我们心不外驰，凡事一门深入，看清事物本质，认清事物真相。一个专一的人能真正做到守信，专一是守信的前提。因此，"无我、利他、专一、守信"这八个字，成就的是：道、术、德。

When it comes to "no ego", we must first understand the concept of "no ego". "No" means nothing, no existence, nihility. "Ego" means self, existence, true and real. In order to be truly altruistic, one must rise to the level of selflessness in thought and action. At this time, the "I" has its own body, but its mind is selfless. It completely lays down all its own interests and whole-heartedly survive for others. This is a prajna intellectual realm: "Empty is color; color is empty."

No ego is the invisible empty, the "tao", and the wholehearted for others means the visible physical. Therefore, Yes - the visible physical is convenience, and No - the invisible empty plays its part. The "visible physical" is our body, and the body carries an unselfish mind. This mind cherishes the world, only the mind of the world, can it has great use. Just as Lao Tzu said, "The saints have no fickle mind, but the minds of the people." Thus the people of the world have achieved the status of the saints through act of genuine altruism.

Just as Ding Yifeng has grown stronger, it is because we have promised to be selfless, honored with selflessness, imparted more benefits and wisdom to everyone, and everyone has realized the greatness of Ding Yifeng.

To say "specialization" again. That is, one is specific, and the so-called specialization is focused on one thing, one person, or one field etc. The specialization is that the mind is pure and the mind is focused to the extreme. Buddhism calls it Zen, and Lao Tzu called it "to the hollow, to be quiet". Only such a clean and focused effort can achieve extraordinary careers. Speciality allows us to keep our minds on the thing, and everything goes deeper, seeing the essence of things, and recognizing the truth of things. Therefore, a specialized person can truly be trustworthy. Specialization is a prerequisite for trustworthiness. Therefore, the words "Selflessness, altruism, specialization, and trustworthiness" are the achievements of Taoism, technique, and morality.

22

论虚拟经济
On virtual economy

佛家有言:"法无定法"
The Buddhist said,
"Law is uncertain"

金融起源于四千多年前的西方,之后随着欧洲历史的发展和变迁,犹太人成为世界金融的主要掌控者。

众所周知,犹太民族是一个智商优异但多灾多难的民族。他们的祖先历经尽千难万险,以耶路撒冷为首都建立了自己的国家——以色列;但仅仅七十年,这个国家就遭遇某些国家和民族的驱赶、打击和压迫。这种灾难深重、无比悲惨的生存状态使得犹太人颠沛流离,居无定所。整整两千年,这个民族在夹缝中生存。由此,犹太人大多不可能选择发展实体经济,于是一个以犹太人为主力的、以钱生钱的金融事业,在西班牙、德国、英国和美国等地相继蓬勃发展起来。犹太人对金融发展起着非同小可的作用,他们掌控着欧洲各国的经济命脉。当今西方的大银行家、大金融家、大资本家基本都是犹太人。创办高盛等的大财团,以及以金融大鳄巴菲特、索罗

斯等为代表的犹太人，操纵着美国 70% 以上的财富。

透过以上现象，我们不难看出，当今世界是一个虚拟经济和实体经济并存的时代。在金融方面，中国还处于弱势；而其中原因就在于以钱生钱的金融，与中国自古以来主张勤劳致富的理念几乎是相对立的。但回到现实，当今中国如果不积极主动地推动虚拟经济的发展，于国于民都将不利。货币战争没有硝烟，弱肉强食是必然的结果。

在中华民族逐渐强大的今天，我们必须遵循老子《道德经》所言："挫其锐，解其纷；和其光，同其尘。"虚拟经济虽然与我们的传统致富理念有些冲突，但它毕竟是强国的手段。所以，我们必须东西融合，才能挫其锐气，解除纷争。

佛家有言："法无定法。"我的理解是：法无正邪，人心有正邪。正如钱币本无正邪，将钱币用在何处才决定正邪。因此，我们用什么样的方法强国利民，全在起心动念。

Finance originated in the West more than 4,000 years ago. Later, with the development and change of European history, the Jewish became the world's major financial controller.

As we all know, the Jewish is an ethnic group with outstanding intelligence but ha suffered many disasters. Their ancestors went through thousands of hardships and set up their country with Jerusalem as their capital: Israel; but only 70 years later, the country was again driven away, attacked, and oppressed by other countries and nations. This kind of catastrophic and extremely tragic state of living has caused the Jews to move away from their homes. Throughout 2,000 years, the nation survived in the cracks. As a result, most Jews are not able to choose the real economy. Therefore, a Jewish-dominated, money-creating financial business has flourished in Spain, Germany, the United Kingdom, and the United States. In 1,500 or so, Jews played a very important role in finance. They controlled the economic lifeline of European countries. Today's big Western bankers, big financiers, and big capitalists are all Jewish. The Jewish-founded Goldman Sachs and other large consortiums, as well as the Jews, represented by financial tycoons such as Buffett and Soros, manipulated more than 70% of U.S. wealth.

Through the above phenomena, we can easily see that today's world is an era in which virtual economy and real economy coexist. In terms of finance, China is still in a weak position. The reason for this trend lies in the fact that finances that use money to produce money are almost in opposition to China's ancient concept of hardworking and wealth. However, returning to reality, if China does not actively promote the development of the virtual economy, it will be unfavorable to the country and the people. In the currency war, "the weak are the prey of the strong" is the inevitable result.

In today's increasingly powerful China, we must follow the Lao Tzu's *Tao Te Ching*: "To kill too prominent front angle, to resolve the tangled contradictions, convergence too dazzling light, all the existence of a whole." Although the virtual economy has some conflicts with our traditional concept of gaining wealth, it is a means of strengthening the country. Therefore, we must integrate the East and West in order to give our people a better life.

The Buddhist said, "Law is uncertain." My understanding is: Law is not inherently good or evil; people have good and evil minds. Just as the stock market is not inherently good or evil. Only when the people use the stock market their intentions could be good or evil. Therefore, what kind of methods we use to strengthen the country, it's all in our mind.

23

论 "心"
On "mind"

万事由心造，万法由心生

Everything is created by the mind,
and all laws are born of the mind

　　从生理上讲，人人都有一颗跳动的心，这个心是心脏。心脏为血液循环提供动力，负责把血液输送到身体各部位。心脏是维系生命不可缺少的重要器官，它是物质方面的心。

　　与此同时，我们还有另一个非物质方面的心，这个心无形无相，无色无味，摸不着，看不见。它以人的躯体为载体，换言之，它就住在我们的身体里。它对人的思维（思想）起着决定性的作用。故圣人老子言："有之以为利，无之以为用。"这里的"有"是我们通过眼睛可以看见的身体，它以肉眼可见的形态而存在并且承载着一个看不见的心。因此，心可以无边无际、无限广大。而身体却有很大局限；身体再大，大不过心。任何有形的事物都有着很大的局限性，只有无形无相，老子称之为"道"的东西，才是不可估量的。无形的道可以生出无量有形之物。于是佛家所说"万般神通皆小术，唯有空空是大道"的含义，就不难理解了。

　　"万事由心造，万法由心生"意思是大千世界的千万种事物、千万种认知事物和解决问题的方法，都是由心所产生的。人因心而各不相同，什么样的心性，决定什么样的人生。

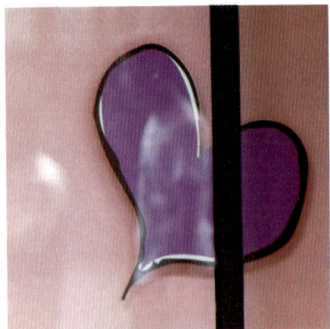

秋言物语

Physically speaking, everyone has one heart and one mind. The heart is a flesh organ beating without stopping. The heart powers the blood circulation and is responsible for delivering blood to all parts of the body. The heart is an indispensable vital organ that sustains life. It is a material heart.

At the same time, we have another non-material mind. The mind is intangible, colorless and invisible. The mind is based in the human body. In other words, it lives in our bodies. It plays a decisive role in people's thinking (ideology). Therefore, sage Lao Tzu remarked, "Yes - the visible physical is convenience, and No - the intangible plays its part." Here "physical" is the body that we can see with our eyes and touch with our hands. It exists in a concret flesh form and carries an invisible mind. Therefore, the mind can be boundless and unlimited. But the flesh body has great limitations. No matter how big the body is, it can not exceed the mind. Any tangible thing has many limitations. Only things that are intangible, Lao Tzu call "Tao", are immeasurable. The invisible Tao can produce immeasurable tangible things. Therefore, the Buddhists say: it is not difficult to understand that "all kinds of supernatural powers are small techniques, and only empty space is the great Tao."

"Everything is created by the mind, and all laws are born of the mind." It means thousands of things in the world, thousands of rules of understanding and answers to problems are all produced by the mind. People are different because of their own minds. What kind of mind, decide what kind of life.

24 ——————————————————————

看"共享单车"有感
Look at "mobike"

秋言物语

执古之道，以御今之有

Using the already existing "Tao" to
control the reality of the concrete things

清晨，当我推开落地窗步入阳台，清新的空气散发着一股植物的芳香，扑面而来，顿时整个身心像被一层美丽的轻纱抱拥，薄而柔……慢慢地，一抹阳光透过对面山上的树梢，暖暖地洒落在身上。于是我蜷缩着坐在木椅上，享受着早晨的美好。

随着思维发散，我脑海里出现了一个个"共享单车"的画面：上班途中，一边是一辆辆骑行在路上的单车，一边却是一辆辆杂乱无序停放在草丛里、花园旁、干道边甚至快速路上的单车。无处不见的共享单车，涂着耀人双目的颜色，形成一处处视觉污染。

在此情形之下，我们不得不思索一个问题，共享单车在给市民带来随手可得的方便之时，又污染了这个美丽的城市。物质文明发展至今，人的意义何在？从机器工业的发展到电子工业的突飞猛进，人类被完全物化了。我们在无数的机器面前丧失了成就感、价值观、道德观，丧失了我们曾经具备的行为能力。更令人吃惊的是，孙正义预测，未来三十年机器人的智商会超过人类。这意味着人类设计了机器人，反之机器人又来设计人类，是忧还是喜？

宇宙空间是多维次的，人类所生存的空间在二维之内。因此，我们这个空间维次的任何事物皆有两面性。苦乐、善恶、好坏、高低等等，这就是一分为二的辩证法，这就是古人所言的阴阳之道。正如共享单车，一方面给人带来便利，另一方面又造成安全隐患和环境混乱。怎样合理地解决好两者之间的矛盾，是我们当下所面临的问题。

　　"执古之道，以御今之有。能知古始，是谓道纪。"早在两千多年前老子就告诉我们：把握了古代的道，就能够驾驭今天的"有"；能够明了古代深远而广大的智慧，这就是道的纲纪。愿共享单车在给市民带来方便的同时，也能成为城市的一道风景。多一份宽容，多一份喜乐。

In the morning, when I pushed open my balcony door and walked into the morning breeze, the fresh air exudes the scent of the plants around me and suddenly my entire body and mind seemed to be calmed. It was light and soft... a gradual touch of sunshine. So I curled up in a wooden chair and enjoyed the beauty of the morning.

As my thoughts diverged, I saw images of rental bicycles: on the way to work, the bike was moving along, but all the way there was the bike strewn about, disorganized, in the grass, next to the garden, next to the main road, even on the tracks of the light rail. The shared bikes were everywhere to be found, full of dirty, in chaotic.

Under these circumstance, we have to think about one problem. When rental bicycles bring convenience to the public, they also pollute this beautiful city. What is the significance of the development of material civilization so far? From the development of the industrial revolution to the rapid advancement of the electronics industry, humanity has been completely materialized. We lost our sense of accomplishment, values, and morality in front of countless machines and lost our ability to perform. Even more surprising is Sun Zhengyi's prediction that the robot's IQ will exceed humanity in the next 30 years; this means that humans have designed robots, and robots have outpaced humans. Is it worry or joy?

Cosmic spaces are multidimensional, and humans are living within two dimensions. Therefore, everything in our dimension space has two sides. Bitterness and joy, goodness and evil, high and low, and so on. This is the dialectical law that divides into two parts. This is what the ancients said about Yin and Yang. Just as renting a city bike, on the one hand, it brings convenience to people. On the other hand, it also causes security risks and environmental chaos. How to properly resolve the contradiction between the two is a problem we face today.

Using the already existing "Tao" to control the reality of the concrete things. To be able to understand the beginning of the universe is called to recognize the law of "Tao". As early as two thousand years ago, Lao Tzu told us that if we grasp the ancient rules, we can control today's "being". We are able to understand the deep and vast wisdom of ancient times. This is the outline of the Tao. It is willing to offer rental bicycles to bring convenience to the citizens, but it can also become a landscape for the city. More tolerance and more joy.

25

了解事物的真相
Know the truth of things

大音希声，大象无形，大器晚成

The great sound is faintly heard;
the great image is invisible;
the great talent takes time to mature

　　总的来说，人们通常会犯一种错，那就是当我们对一件事物的认识并不清晰和透彻的时候，往往误以为自己已经懂了。其实人们对事物的认识程度，通过听其言而观其行便可知晓。

　　我个人认为对事物的认识有三个阶段：初级阶段是见闻，也就是听说和看见，这个阶段对事物仅仅达到表象的认识，离事物的真实情况相差甚远；中级阶段是对事物的认识透过表象和初步的实践，已触摸到事物的本质；高级阶段是通过实践和认识、再实践再认识的不断深入，而逐渐透彻了解事物的真相。因此圣人老子言："大音希声，大象无形，大器晚成。"

　　大音希声的意思是无比强大的音声是听不到的，好比宇宙浩瀚无际，但我们听不见它有什么声音。反之雷声很大，但其音响是有限的，如同在深圳听不见北京的雷声。

大象无形比喻时空如同虚空一样，无始无终，无边无际。无论我们用什么样的方法，也不能测度时间与空间的长度和宽度。时间、空间以无形的状态而存在。

大器晚成：一个真正成功的人，对客观事物的认识，是建立在不断探索研究，以及勤奋勇敢、艰苦卓绝的认知实践之上的。正如先师孔子所言："三十而立，四十不惑，五十知天命。"知天命者而大成。

秋言物语

In general, people often make a mistake, that is, when we do not understand something clearly and thoroughly, we often mistakenly believe that we have already understand it. In fact, people's understanding of things can be seen by listening to their words and observing their behavior.

Personally, I think there are three stages in understanding things: First is knowledge, which can be heard and seen. At this stage, the understanding of things only reaches the appearance, which is far from the true situation of things. Second, the intermediate stage is the understanding of things through the appearance and preliminary practice. It has touched the essence of things. Third, in the advanced stage, through the continuous deepening of practice and understanding, through practice and understanding, the truth of things has gradually become clear. Therefore, the Saint Lao Tzu said, "The great sound is faintly heard; the great image is invisible; the great talent takes time to mature."

The great sound is faintly heard: The meaning is that extremely powerful sounds can hardly be heard. It is like the vastness of the universe, but we can't hear what it sounds like. On the contrary, the thunder is very loud, but its sound is limited and gone in a flash.

The great image is invisible: It is time and space, no beginning, no end and no limits. No matter what method we use, we cannot measure the length and width of time and space. Time and space exist in an invisible state.

The great talent takes time to mature: A truly successful person, his understanding of objective things is based on constant exploration and research, as well as diligent, courageous and arduous practice. As the first Teacher Confucius said, "man at thirty can afford, forty not be bewitched, fifty knows one's fate." Knowing the destiny is a saint.

26

小学时代的精神内核
My spiritual core at elementary school

佛说当下即未来
Buddhist says the moment
is the future

　　在我年幼的时候，记得那时没有学前班，孩童年满7岁上小学一年级，而我却是个例外。"文化大革命"期间，阶级斗争很激烈，我们一家四口居无定所，由此耽误了我上学的最佳时间。

　　记得11岁那年，母亲才带我去报名入学。11岁按理应该上小学四年级，而我却很尴尬地上三年级。不识字，不会拼音，更不会算术，那时我整个状况像白痴一样。那个年代，我能在学校留下来学习，是因为我会唱样板戏，会跳《白毛女》；我虽不识字，但也会背诵"老三篇"，同时还以"椒盐普通话"当上了学校的报幕员，也就是今天的主持人。整个小学时代就这样懵懵懂懂地过去了……这导致我至今不会拼音，提笔写错别字成了家常便饭。印象深刻的是父亲给了我一个"错别字大王"的绰号。这就是我真实的童年。

　　佛说当下即未来，意思是今天的行为决定未来的状况。人生的每

一段经历都在得失之间。在那个特殊的年代，我虽然缺失了基础知识的教育，但毛主席的"老三篇"在我灵魂深处埋下了不灭的种子。

《为人民服务》纪念的张思德，为人民的利益而死，比泰山还重。毛主席引用了司马迁的名言："人固有一死，或重于泰山，或轻于鸿毛。"

《愚公移山》："下定决心，不怕牺牲，排除万难，去争取胜利！"愚公用子子孙孙挖山不止的精神感动了天神，天神派神仙把两座大山背走了。

《纪念白求恩》：一位五十多岁的医生，为了中国人民的解放事业，不远万里从加拿大来到中国，用生命谱写了一首"毫不利己、专门利人"的影响时代的精神赞歌！

这就是那个时代留给我最为珍贵的精神内核，这种无我利他的思想，铸就了中华民族的伟大与非凡！

When I was young, I did not attend elementary school. Usually, when a child is 7 years old, he would be in first grade. I was an exception. During "the Cultural Revolution", the class struggle was very fierce. Our family of four had no fixed place to live. This delayed the time for me to go to school.

I remember when I was 11 years old, my mother took me to the primary school to enroll. A girl at 11-year-old should be in fourth grade in elementary school, but I was very embarrassed in Grade Three. I couldn't read, couldn't spell, couldn't count, I was like an idiot. In those days, I could stay and study in the school because I could sing in the school play *White Haired Girl*; I could not read, but I could recite. The whole primary school years have passed in such a daze. I never learned to write in elementary school and spelling mistakes become a daily occurrence. What impressed me most is that my father gave me a nickname "misnomer". This is my real childhood.

Buddhist says the moment is the future. It means that today's actions determine the future. Every experience in life is between gains and losses. In that particular era, although I had lost the basic knowledge of education, but Chairman Mao's "Three Constantly Read Articles" planted the seeds of eternal in my soul.

Serve the People commemorates Zhang Side, who died for the benefit of the people, a burden heavier than Mount Tai. Chairman Mao quoted Si Maqian's famous saying, "Man is born to die, whether he is heavier than Mount Tai, or lighter than a feather."

Yu Gong Moves Mountain: "To make up your mind, not to fear sacrifice, to eliminate all difficulties, to fight for victory!" Yu

Gong dug the mountains with the spirit of digging by his children constantly one generation after the other, his spirit touched the God and the God sent the immortals to move away the two mountains.

Memorial to Bethune: A doctor in his fifties traveled thousands of miles from Canada to China for the sake of the Chinese people's liberation cause. He wrote with his life a spiritual hymn "be not selfish, be for the people" that has influenced and affected generations.

This is the most precious spiritual core that was left to me in that era. This kind of thinking without self-interest created the greatness and extraordinariness of the Chinese nation!

27

《心经》的感悟

Heart Sutra Enlightenment

色即是空，空即是色，受想行识，亦复如是

Color is empty, empty is color, feelings,
thoughts, actions, perceptions are all the same

歌手王菲的歌曲广为流传，在她唱的众多歌曲中，我唯一感兴趣，也是唯一能记住歌名和歌词的就是《心经》。

《心经》是佛家经典，其全称为《般若波罗蜜多心经》。

"般若"（bō rě），是梵语智慧的意思，般若智慧是一种明白了宇宙人生所有真理的智慧境界。佛学称之为"了了分明"，凡事一目了然。"波罗蜜"是到达彼岸的意思，也就是说此岸是凡夫，彼岸是觉悟了真理的人（佛）；从凡夫通过修行而到达了佛的智慧境界。所以佛是觉悟的人，人是迷惑的众生。

《心经》指出：从凡夫到佛的过程是用心修成的，而并非依赖眼、耳、鼻、舌、身、意六根，以及对应六根的色、声、香、味、

触、法六尘而修成的。一切人所具备的眼界、意识界、无明界、生老病死界、苦难界以及得失等等，都是到达彼岸的障碍。相反，我们只能通过修行逐渐忘却人的本质，从而进入道的范畴。所以得道的人说："顺者成人，逆者成仙。"

"色不异空，空不异色，色即是空，空即是色。"这句话很难理解。空是无的意思，色是有的意思。执着于无和执着于有都不是成道的方法。空与色、有与无在凡夫眼里是二，而在得道人看来只是一。因此，佛学称不二法门，空色、有无皆为一。所以，"色即是空，空即是色，受想行识，亦复如是"。

The songs of Singer Faye Wong is widely circulated. Among the many songs she sang, I am only interested in the *Heart Sutra*.

The *Heart Sutra* is a Buddhist classic. Its whole name called the *Prajna Paramita Heart Sutra*. "Prajna" is the meaning of Sanskrit wisdom. Prajna wisdom is a state of wisdom that understands all the truths of the universe and the human life. Buddhism called it "clear", and everything is clear at a glance. "Paramita" means to reach the other side, that is to say on this shore is a mortal, and on the other side is a person who has realized the truth (Buddha); the mortal, through practice, is trying to reach Buddha, to learn his wisdom. The Buddha is a person of enlightenment and the goal of the mortal.

The *Heart Sutra* points out that the process from the mortal to the Buddha is done with the mind, not rely on the six senses: not with the eyes, ears, nose, tongue, body, and sense, as well as the six dusts corresponding to the six senses: the color, sound, fragrance, taste, touch, and method. The vision, the consciousness, the ignorance, the sickness and death, the suffering, and the gains and losses of all people are all obstacles to reaching the other side. On the contrary, we can only enter another realm of Tao by gradually

gaining back the forgotten human nature through practice. So the one who got the Tao said, "The obedient adult, the rebellious become immortal."

It is different to understand the following phrase: "The color is not different, empty is not different, the color is empty, the empty is color." The empty is the meaning of none, the color is the material form. Persistence in "empty" form is not a method of enlightenment. Empty and color, yes and no, they are two in the eyes of the moral, but in the eyes of the Taoist is only one. Therefore, Buddhism holds two as one. The empty, color, yes or no are the same as one. Therefore, color is empty, empty is color, feelings, thoughts, actions, perceptions are all the same.

28 ————————————————————

晨起登高一览物，山河草木汇城池

The mountain, river, grassland and town in the morning

我仿佛听到了宇宙的声音，又仿佛看见了我灵魂的归宿

I seem to have heard the voice of the universe,
and it seems that I have seen the ownership of my soul

清晨五点，天光未现。借着灯光，我乘电梯登上了五十多层的大楼顶层。形单影只，脚踩大楼，眼望四周。啊！这情景如同启动手机微信出现的那个画面。此刻我就像独自站在地球上……

我仿佛听到了宇宙的声音，又仿佛看见了我灵魂的归宿。"摩诃般若波罗蜜，摩诃般若波罗蜜……"我不由自主地在心里重复默念着这句佛语。

"摩诃"是广大的意思，心量广大，犹如虚空，无上下长短，无喜乐忧伤，无是也无非，无善也无恶，无始也无终，这就是虚空法界。

太阳东升西落，明暗交替。暗因明成，明因暗显。有与无，色与空，动与静，曲与直，明理者当立于非暗非明之中道。

般若智慧人人具有，只是心迷而不能自悟。愚人、智人，其佛性本无差别，只是迷悟不同。破迷开悟，方得解脱。"有信仰的愚昧

无知，无信仰的博学多才"，这两者都不可取。佛是什么？佛是觉悟的人。佛是道德、慈悲、智慧的代名词。

Five o'clock in the morning, before the light of the sky has yet to appear, I boarded the elevator to the top of a 50-story building. Only my solitary footsteps echoes through out the building. Looking around. Ah! This scene is similar to the one in which mobile WeChat appears - a man looking at Earth. At the moment, I'm just like standing alone on the earth...

I seem to have heard the voice of the universe, and it seems that I have seen the ownership of my soul. "The Mahabana Prajnaparam, the Maha Prajnaparam..." I couldn't help but repeat the mantra in my heart.

"Maha" is a broad meaning. It is like a void, no length, no joy or sorrow, nothing more than nothingness. There is no good and no evil. There is no beginning nor end. This is the realm of the void.

The sun rises in the east and goes down in the west; light and dark alternate. The darkness is due to bright, and bright due to darkness. There are form and nothingness, color and emptiness, moving and static, bending and straight; a wise man will take a way between non-darkness and non-clarity.

The wise people all have Prajna, only the confused cannot realize it yet themselves. The fools and clever, have no difference in Buddha's nature. The difference is only fascination and enlightenment. Breaking confusion and having enlightenment, you can be free. "Those who have faith are foolish and ignorant, and those who do not believe are erudite," neither of which is desirable. What is Buddha? Buddha is the enlightened person. The Buddha is synonymous of morality, compassion, and wisdom.

感悟"戒、定、慧"

Inspiration of "commandments, meditation and wisdom"

我们今天到底是进步了还是后退了

Today are we progressing
or regressing

清晨五时，天光未现，手按开关，房灯亮起。刹那间，思绪被灯的光亮引发……

在佛学中，我们常常可以看见"戒、定、慧"三个字。"戒"指的是：一不杀生（亲自杀和间接杀）；二不偷盗（不取不义之财物，不探他人之秘密）；三不邪淫（夫妻之外的不正当男女关系，以及意念之不正当的想法）；四不妄语（不说谎话，不说狂傲之语）。只有把持戒律，才能生发定力。"定"指的是专一、专注，心不外驰，心神合一，知行合一。长此以往"戒定"成为自然而然的行为。

这时"戒定"的力量方能开启智慧的大门。

　　写到这里，我由衷地感到，现代文字（白话文）的力不从心！大道至简，现代文字，不知从什么时候开始变到如此复杂的地步。古代经典所言："智慧观照，内外明彻。识自本心，若识本心，即本解脱。若得解脱，即得三昧。"如此简单、明了、透彻的古代文字，当今的我们却难以理解。我不禁哀叹，今天的我们到底是进步了还是后退了？

　　戒、定、慧，就像灯光一样，有灯即有光，无灯即黑暗。灯是光的身体，光是灯的用处。虽然名为灯光，一灯、二光，但灯光同一。戒、定、慧的方法亦复如是。

Five o'clock in the morning, before the light of the sky has yet to appear, I pressed my hand on the light switch and the room flooded with light. In a flash, thoughts are lightened by the lamp.

In Buddhism, we can often see the characters "Jie, Ding, Hui". "Jie" means commandments; "Ding" means meditation; Hui means wisdom. "Jie" refers to: 1. do not kill; 2. do not steal (whether it be physical goods or secrets of others); 3. do not engage in sexual prostitution (unfair relationship between men and women, and unfair ideas that are not justified); 4. Do not lie (or speak the language of arrogance). Only by holding the commandments can we rise in meditation. "Meditation" refers to the oneness and concentration, the mind does not push, the mind is united, and the knowledge and practice are united. In the long term, "Jie, Ding" have become a natural behavior. At this time, the power of "Jie, Ding" can open the door to wisdom.

After writing this, I sincerely feel that the power of my modern text (in Chinese) is not good! The Tao is very simple, but modern writing, I do not know when it began to change to such a complicated point. The ancient scriptures said, "Look inside intelligently at your mind, both inside and outside are clear; if you realize your own nature, you are free. If you have to be free, you will get Samādhi-Suspend all distractions, calm the mind." It is so simple, clear and thorough in ancient text, but it is difficult for us today to understand. I could not help but sigh, today, are we progressing or regressing?

"Jie, Ding, Hui" are just like lights. There are lights; there is light. No lights, it is dark. The lamp is the light body, and the light is the use of the lamp. Although the name is the light of the lamp, one lamp, two light, but the light of lamp are one. The methods of "Jie, Ding, Hui" are also the same.

秋言物语

30

《易经》感悟
Inspiration of the *I-Ching*

《易经》乃天人合一之作

The *I-Ching* is
a combination of nature and humanity

在刚刚结束的禅道商学院"元丰计划"课程上，院方给优秀学员颁发了一本《易经》，以兹鼓励和激发学员的向学之心。

在此我怀着一颗学习的心态，来跟大家分享我对《易经》的一点粗浅认识。

《易经》又名《周易》，为什么呢？据说在六千多年前的上古时代，我们的始祖伏羲根据大自然的种种物象，用八卦把自然和人的关系表示出来，八卦代表人与自然的法则。之后三千多年，周文王根据当时的社会现象和商纣王治理国家的弊端，又将八卦演变为六十四卦。故《易经》又名《周易》。继周朝之后，孔子做《易传》，先师把宇宙秩序和人生规律更加紧密地连接起来，并强调了道德实践的重要性。于是在长达三千五百多年的时间里，三位圣人完成了这部千古不朽的辉煌之作！

《易经》到底讲的是什么呢？八卦以及六十四卦又是什么意思呢？有人说《易经》是用来占卜、预测、相面、算命的；有人说

《易经》是用来行医的，医易同源；还有人说《易经》是一部最古老、最完美的哲学著作。更为神奇的是，在出土的远古印第安人的一个彩钵上，竟有《易经》的"复卦"，以至考古学家们不禁在内心发问，难道印第安人的祖先是中国人？众所周知，微积分发明人之一的莱布尼兹从《易经》中获得启发，发明了一套"二进制"法则，成为计算机语言的理论基础。不仅如此，生物学家又发现DNA脱氧核糖核酸的遗传密码，不多不少正好六十四个。这些密码破译之后，恰恰是一组完整的六十四卦的排列次序。这难道是巧合吗？

所以，我只能惊叹！面对《易经》，我们凡夫俗子是多么的渺小和无知……《易经》乃天人合一之作，它以德为本，能令人趋吉避凶，它能精准定位，它能永续长存。

At the just concluded course of the "Yuanfeng Plan" at the Zen Tao Business School, the school awarded the excellent student the *I-Ching* so as to encourage and enhance the student's mind toward learning.

Here, with a learning attitude, I would like to share with you some of my initial understanding of the *I-Ching*.

The *I-Ching* is also known as the *Book of Changes*. Why? It is said that over 6,000 years ago in ancient times, Fu Xi, a Chinese cultural ancestor, used the Gossip to express the relationship between the nature and people based on various natural phenomena. Gossip represents the law of the nature and the human beings.

About three thousand years later, the king Wen of the Zhou Dynasty, according to the social phenomenon of the time and the malpractice of Shang king zhou to govern the country, turned the Gossip into sixty-four hexagrams. Therefore, the *I-Ching* is also known as the *Book of Changes*. After the Zhou Dynasty, Confucius made *Yi Zhuan* to connect the cosmic order and the law of life more closely, and emphasized the importance of moral practice. So for more than 3,500 years, the three saints completed this eternal glory!

What exactly does the *Book of Changes* talk about? What is the meaning of Gossip and sixty-four hexagrams? Some people say that the *Book of Changes* is used for divining, forecasting, face reading, and fortune-telling; some people say that the Book of Changes is used to practice medicine, the *Book of Changes* and medicine have the same root; others also say that the *Book of Changes* is the oldest and most perfect Philosophical writings. What is even more amazing is that, on a color bowl of ancient unearthed Indians, there is a "Fu hexagram" of the *Book of Changes*, so that archaeologists could not help but question their minds. Is it that the ancestors of the Indians were Chinese? It is well known that Leibniz, one of the inventors of differential and integral calculus, was inspired by the *Book of Changes* and invented a set of "binary" rules that became the theoretical basis of computer languages. Not only that, biologists also found that the genetic codes of DNA are exactly 64. After these codes were deciphered, it was precisely the complete sequence of the orders of the sixty-four hexagrams. Is this coincidence?

In summary, I can only marvel! In the face of the *Book of Changes*, how ordinary and ignorant we mortals are. The *Book of Changes* is a combination of nature and humanity. It is based on virtue, and it can be used to the auspicious and to ward off the evil. It can be precisely positioned. It can operate forever.

31

爱情的感悟
Feelings of love

世上没有无缘无故的爱，也没有无缘无故的恨

There is no love for no reason at all,
and there is also no hate for no reason

随着法国总统大选的尘埃落定，马卡龙这个令世界震惊的传奇人物，在世界政治舞台上大放异彩。与此同时，伴随着他的睿智、才能，以及英俊的外形，马先生的妻子，一位把学生培养成丈夫，又把丈夫培养成总统的女人，同样引起世界的瞩目。在世俗人眼里，

布丽吉特大她的丈夫24岁，并且是3个孩子的母亲、7个孙子的奶奶，人们就她这种年龄和形象上的落差，发出了五花八门的疑问。在此我只想说说自己的一点看法。

就爱情而言，人世间有多少个人，就有多少种爱情。没有哪一个人的爱情可以成为一个标准，也没有哪一个人的爱情方式可以成为一个固定的模式。爱情世界是一个自由的王国，芸芸众生在这个国度里，自由地续接自己的因缘。毛主席说过："世上没有无缘无故的爱，也没有无缘无故的恨。"这句话也充分地说明，世间万事万物，都不能脱离"因缘"（因果）二字。夫妻是累生累世的因缘果报。世间万事万物无一不在缘生缘灭中轮回。只有我们明白了这一道理时，我们才能真正看清事物的实相。"实相"二字代表事物的真实不二。

虽然看到马先生和妻子的年龄落差这一现象，但我们无法走进他们的精神世界。我们所看到的现象，远远不是事物的本质。透过这一现象，我们更应该看到马先生人生的辉煌来源于他的人生追求，他的政治抱负能够得以实现并非偶然，因为他从小品学兼优、有理想、有追求。在和布丽吉特建立了情侣关系之后，他兑现了自己的承诺："我一定会回来娶你的。"这就是才华、品德、信誉的落地。

As the dust of the presidential election in France settled down, Mr. Ma, the legendary figure who shocked the world, shined on the world political stage. At the same time, along with his wisdom, talent, and handsome appearance, Mr. Ma's wife, a woman who cultivated her student into a husband and raised her husband into a president, also caught the attention of the world. In the secular eyes, Brigitte's is 24 years older than her husband, and is the mother of three children, and the grandmother of seven grandchildren. People have asked various questions about her age and difference in image. I just want to talk about my own point of view here.

As far as love is concerned, there are as many individuals as there are loves of the people in the world. No one's love can become a standard, and no one's love can become a fixed model. The world of love is a free kingdom, where all sentient beings are free to continue their own causes. Chairman Mao said, "There is no love for no reason at all, and there is also no hate for no reason." This sentence also fully shows that everything in the world cannot be separated from the word "cause" (cause and effect). Husband and wife are a result of a lifetime. All things in the world are in a cycle of birth and death. When we understand this truth, we can really see the reality of things. The word "reality" represents the truth of things.

Although we can see the phenomenon of the age difference between Mr. Ma and his wife, we cannot walk into their spiritual world and soul. The phenomenon we have touched is far from the essence of things. Through this phenomenon, we should also see that Mr. Ma's life's glory comes from his pursuit of life. His political ambition can be realized. It is not accidental because he was an excellent student, he has the ideal and the pursuit. After establishing a love relationship with Brigitte, he fulfilled his promise, "I will definitely come back to marry you." This is where talent, virtue, and credibility are grounded.

32

如何 "趋吉避凶"

How to "take good fortune
away from the evil"

天行健，君子以自强不息；地势坤，君子以厚德载物

As nature's movement is ever vigorous,
so must a gentleman keep improving himself;
as the earth is strong and vast,
so must a gentleman be generous and tolerant to bear all things

　　"趋吉避凶"这个词我们常常说起，但怎样才能做到"趋吉避凶"，我想很多人都无从知晓。

　　古圣先贤除了告诉我们"积善之家必有余庆，积不善之家必有余殃"，还告诉我们"祸福无门，唯人自招"。这些话都明确地指出吉与凶是事物从起因到结果的过程。但人们往往只会看事物的结果，而不能看到事物的起因。我们长期处在"知其然，而不知其所以然"的状态。

　　例如，夫妻之道。从伦理道德上讲，夫妻之道乃乾坤之道。乾为天，坤为地；乾为男，坤为女。换言之，夫为天，妇为地。《易经》有言："天行健，君子以自强不息；地势坤，君子以厚德载物。"这就是乾坤定位，这就是男女平等。平等的地位，不同的属性！而

现代人却大肆强调男女平等，往往忽略了男女不同的属性！

　　一个家庭，丈夫为天，妻子为地。丈夫要效仿天，自强不息，周而复始；妻子要效仿大地，厚德载物，包容和承载，即使能力大过丈夫，也要在心性和品质上守护着丈夫的地位。如果想掌控丈夫，那就是倒反天纲，错乱伦常，必有灾祸发生。

　　因此，如何趋吉避凶？从人道的伦理道德开始，从夫妻的乾坤之道开始，从而悟得天地不灭的真谛！

We often talk about the phrase "get for good fortune away from the evil", but how can we really get it. I think a lot of people do not know how to really achieve it.

Ancient saints not only told us "A family that accumulates merits is bound to have extending blessings, while a family that continues to do evils is doomed to have endless disasters.", but also told us also that "there is no door for the evil or good, and only one person can recruit himself." These words clearly indicate that good and evil are the processes of things from the cause to the result. People will often only see the results of things, but not the causes of the results of things. We have long been in a state of knowing it, but rather than knowing why it is.

For example, the way of husband and wife. Ethically speaking, the way of husband and wife is the way of the heaven and the earth. The Chinese character "qian"(乾) means the heaven, "kun"(坤) means the earth. Qian stands for male; kun stands for female. In other words, husband is the heaven and wife is the earth. The *Book of Changes* has said, "As nature's movement is ever vigorous, so must a gentleman keep improving himself; as the earth is strong and vast, so must a gentleman be generous and tolerant to bear all things." This is the position of the heaven and the earth. This is the equality of men and women. The equal status, the different attributes! Modern people, however, emphatically emphasize equality between men and women, and often overlook the different attributes of men and women!

In a family, husband is the heaven and the wife is the earth. The husband should follow the example of the nature and strive for self- improvement. The wife should imitate the earth, cherish the virtues, embrace and carry the burden. Even if her ability is greater than that of her husband, she must protect her husband's position on the nature and quality. If you want to master and control your husband, it is to rebel against the nature. If you violate the law of the nature and morality, thus disasters are doomed to follow.

Therefore, how to get for good fortune away from the evil? Starting from the moral ethics of humanity, and from the way of husband and wife, so as to realize the undying truth of the heavens and the earth truthfully!

33

人是什么
What is human?

人为何物？这一问题要具备怎样的智慧才可以解答？
What is the man, what wisdom does this question need to
have to be answered

看到一篇文章在谈论"人是什么"，并这样写到——

物理学家说：人是碳原子的产物。

生物化学家说：人是核酸酶的相互作用器。

生物学家说：人是细胞的聚集体。

天文学家说：人是星河的孩子。

人类学家说：两足的出现，敏锐的目光，勤劳的双手……

众说纷纭，各执所见。

在我看来，以上知见都是局部的了解，都不是事物的真相。是啊！浩瀚宇宙，人为何物？这一问题要具备怎样的智慧才可以解答？从佛家经典中，我们可以明白"人"是不明真理的产物。从入胎到脱胎成为人之后，我们便不断地重复着昨天的故事。正因为有了前世一个不明真相的我们，才有了如今一个个仍然不明真相的我们。

整个人类世界，大家共业共缘，共同来到这个"大同世界"。共同的业力，造就了共同的因缘，我们带着妄想、分别、执着会聚在地球上，又不断地重复着妄想、分别、执着。如此循环往复，周而复始。这就是人类生生不息的本源。

我们不具备究竟圆满的智慧德能，因此我们不能彻底看清事物的真正实相。于是带着妄想、分别、执着，硬生生地打造了一个苦多乐少，或者说一个苦乐参半的人的世界。即使这样，我们却还是全然不知！

因此，圣贤教育不可或缺。经典之所以万古流传，是那些极少数觉悟了真理的圣者和跟随圣者的贤人志士来传承和发扬的。

See an article talking about "what is human?" It says----

Physicists say that human is the product of carbon atoms.

Biochemists say that humans are the interactors of nucleic acid enzymes. The biologists say that human beings are the aggregates of cells.

The astronomers said, human is the children of the star river.

The anthropologists said, the appearance of two feet, the sharp eyes, the hard-working hands... And so on.

There are a lot of opinions among people.

In my opinion, the above knowledge is a partial understanding, and it is not the truth of things. -Yeah! Great universe, what is the man? What wisdom does this question need to have to be answered? From the Buddhist scriptures, we can understand that "man" is the product of unknown truth. After entering the womb and becoming a human being, we keep repeating the story of yesterday. It is because we have an unknown truth in the past life that we have one of us who still do not know the truth. In the entire human world, we all share a common relationship and come to this "Common World". Common Karma creates a common cause. We gather on the earth with delusion, parting, and persistence, and we repeat delusion, parting, and persistence. This cycle repeats itself, over and over again. This is the origin of human cieculation.

We do not have the wisdom and virtue of perfection, so we cannot see the real truth of things. So with the delusion, the parting, the persistence, it is just to create a world with more bitter than sweet, or a bittersweet people's world. Even so, we do not know at all!

Therefore, the education of sages is an indispensable education for mankind. The reason why the classics are circulated throughout the ages is that the few saints who have realized the truth and the sages who follow the saints have passed on and carried forward.

34

事物的成、住、坏、空
Generating, growing, deteriorating

人世间万事万物，无时无刻不在发生着变化
All things happen in the world, changing all the time

  通过学习佛家经典，我们明白了"人生在世，世事无常"的道理。人世间万事万物，无时无刻不在发生着变化，而这种变化都遵循着成、住、坏、空的规律。

  所谓成、住、坏、空，是指事物从产生到灭亡的过程，从缘起到缘灭的经历。为此，在《道德经》第一章中，老子清楚而透彻地告诉我们："道可道，非常道；名可名，非常名。"宇宙间有一个万能的"东西"，无始无终地存在于大自然当中。这个"东西"既可以生育天地，又可以运行日月，还可以长养万物。但这个如此强大的"东西"，我们不知道它叫什么名字，

只能牵强地取名为"道"。道如同虚空，涵养万物而不自有。因此，道是宇宙间唯一长久存续的，如同虚空一样，任何力量也无法将虚空毁灭。这就是佛家所说的"空性"的道理。

所以，圣人早就将人生的目标和方向告诉了我们，我们无智的众生只要遵照执行就可以了。

正如当今著名的中国科学院院士朱清时教授在他的退休演讲中所说："当科学家一路坎坎坷坷地爬到山顶、引以为傲的时候，却发现那些开悟的宗教大师早就在山顶等候我们了。"

Through the study of the Buddhist classics, we understand the truth that "the human life is impermanent and the world things are impermanent". All things happen in the world, changing all the time, and this change follows the laws of the generating, growing, deteriorating and empty.

The so-called "Generating, growing, deteriorating and empty" refer to the process from the birth to the demise of things, start from the reason to the cause disappeared. For this reason, in the first chapter of the *Tao Te Ching*, Lao Tzu told us clearly and thoroughly, "Tao" can be expressed in words. It is not an ordinary "dao"; "Name" can also be explained, it is not ordinary "name". There is a universal "thing" in the universe, and it is in nature without a beginning or end. This "thing" can not only give birth to the world, but also can run the sun and the moon, and can grow everything. But this so powerful "thing", we do not know what name it is called, it can only be strongly named "Tao." which contains all things but does not have its own. Therefore, Tao is the only long-lasting and unbreakable thing in the universe, just like the void, no power can destroy the void. This is what the Buddhists call "emptiness".

So the saints have already told us about the goals and direction of the human life, and our unintelligent beings can only follow the implementation.

As Professor Zhu Qingshi, a renowned academician of the Chinese Academy of Sciences, said in his retiring speech, "When scientists proudly climbed to the top of the mountain, proud of them, they found that the religious masters of enlightenment were already at the top of the mountain, waiting for us long before."As Professor Zhu Qingshi, a renowned academician of the Chinese Academy of Sciences, said in his retiring speech, "When scientists proudly climbed to the top of the mountain, proud of them, they found that the religious masters of enlightenment were already at the top of the mountain, waiting for us long before."

35 ────────────────────

病由心生，病由心灭
Disease comes from mind
and is extinguished by mind

疾病的形成都是心造成的，都是由心所导向的结果
The formation of the disease is caused by the mind,
which is the result of the mind-oriented

从某种意义上说，身体的健康与否决定寿命的长短。每个人都想拥有健康的身体、长久的寿命。

然而人究竟怎样才能真正获得健康长寿呢？曾经看到一段文字这样写道："世界卫生组织总结出人的健康有三个因素：心理的健康；身体的健康；与人友好相处。"在我看来，这三个因素仍然是知其然，而不知其所以然。

心理怎样才能真正的健康，这才是问题的关键。佛家一语道破天机："万病由心生，万法由心造。"心，是情绪的主导，怨、恨、恼、怒、烦、贪、嗔、痴、邪、慢，这些不良情绪都是疾病的因。

《黄帝内经》就告诫我们说："思伤脾、忧伤肺、喜伤心、恐伤肾。"这些都是疾病的缘起。

一个贪字，让我们"病从口入"：现代人吃喝太多、太杂。因此，老子告诉我们"余食赘行"，意思是疾病、肥胖这些令我们讨厌的东西，都是吃出来的。所以，"菩萨畏因，凡夫畏果"。觉悟的人都从因上下功夫，不造病因，防患于未然；无智的人则从果上下功夫，疾病形成了再找方法。晚矣！

因此，疾病的形成都是心造成的，都是由心所导向的结果。既然病由心生，我们就要注重每一个当下的心性修养，心底无私天地宽。"无我、利他、专一、守信"同样是治病的良方。病由心生，病由心灭！

In a sense, the health of the body determines the length of life. Everyone wants to have a healthy body and long life.

However, how can people really get healthy and longevity? There was a paragraph of text that read: "The World Health Organization has concluded that there are three factors in human health: First, psychological health; second, physical health; third, being friendly with people." In my opinion, these three factors are still known, but I do not know why.

How can the mental health be truly healthy? This is the key to the problem. The Buddhist saying breaks the mystery: "The disease is caused by the mind, and all laws are created by the mind."

The mind is the dominant emotion: Complaining, hating, trouble, anger, boredom, greed, displeasure, ignorance, evil, arrogance, these unpleasant negative emotions are the causes of the diseases. The *Huang Di Nei Jing* has warned us that "Sorrow hurts the spleen; over grief hurts the lung; over joy hurts the heart, and over panic hurts the kidneys" are the origins of the disease.

One word "greedy" lets us know "Disease comes from the mouth": modern people eat and drink too much, too miscellaneous. Therefore, Lao Tzu told us that "Eating too much is not conducive to action, bringing a burden to the action", which means that diseases and obesity that we hate are all eaten. Therefore, "Buddha fears the cause, and ordinary people fear the result." The awakened men work on cause, do not make the cause of the disease, prevent the disease from the being. Those who don't have wisdom work hard on the result, when the disease forms, they try to find a way to eliminate it, which is too late!

Therefore, the formation of the disease is caused by the mind, which is the result of the mind-oriented. Since the disease is caused by mind, we must pay attention to a current self-cultivation of self-discipline. The selflesness make open mind. "Selflessness, altruism, speciality, and trustworthiness" are also good prescription to cure. The disease is caused by the mind and it is also extinguished by the mind!

36

真理的真正含义

The true meaning of the truth

何为真理？我们追求真理的目的是什么？

What is truth,
what is the purpose that we pursue the truth

真理二字是我们常常谈起。但什么是真理？真理的真正含义是什么？以及我们追求真理的目的是什么？

其实智慧的佛陀在经典中清楚地告诉了我们，真理是宇宙人生的真正实相，也就是宇宙人生的本来面目。并且这种真实之相是不以人的意志为转移的，在任何时候，任何情况下都是：本来如此，必然如此，永远如此。它经得起任何的考验和求证，是亘古不变的！

因此，真理不是谁发明创造的，真理是宇宙人生的本来面目，是佛陀通过审慎的观察、体悟、实证后发现的真实之相，佛陀只是如实地讲述出来而已。

那么明了真理的目的是什么呢？在此举例说明：凡人都有老、病、死三种苦，这就是凡夫俗子。但佛陀通过他审慎的观察，发现人是完全可以从老、病、死这三种苦中解脱出来的，并且佛陀把怎样解脱的方法都讲得非常清楚。我们无智众生只要信受奉行，就可以从老、病、死这三种苦中解脱出来，从而真正获得幸福美满的人生！这才是真正意义上的解脱之道。

The truth is what we often talk about, but what is truth? What is the true meaning of the truth? What is the purpose that we pursue the truth?

In fact, the great Buddha clearly told us in the classics that the truth is the true reality of the universe and life, which is the true face of the universe and humans. And this true aspect is not to be diverted by human's will. At any time and under any circumstances: it is always the case, it must be so, and it will always be. It can stand up to any test and confirmation, and it is invariable forever!

Therefore, the truth is not who invented and created. The truth is the original face of the universe. It is Buddha's real phase discovered through careful observation, comprehension, and demonstration. The Buddha just stated it truthfully.

So what is the purpose of understanding the truth? Here is an example: Everyone has three kinds of bitterness: old, sick, and dead. This is the mortal. However, through his careful observation, the Buddha found that people can be completely free from old age, illness, and suffering. The Buddha's method of liberation is very clear. As long as our unintelegent mortals are faithfully following, we can free ourselves from old age, sickness, and suffering, so that we can truly have a happy and perfectly satisfactory life! This is the true sense of relief.

37

杀生的业力
Killing karma

欲知世上刀兵劫，但听夜半屠门声

Would like to know the swordsman robbers in the world and listen to the sound of the slaughter in the middle of the night

今天，一位下属告诉我，现在好多人在餐桌上杀生，贪享口腹之欲。是的，这种现象随处可见。当今大多数人的饮食都是荤食居多、素食甚少。面对这样一种极为普遍现象，我认为这是众生的业力所致。

所谓业力，是指人在从事善业或恶业的过程中所形成的一种无形的力量，而这种力量会牵引着我们去到善处，或者去到恶处（也就是种善因得善果、种恶因得恶果的关系）。

荤食是以杀生为代价的恶业力，这其中有间接杀生和直接杀生

两种行为：间接杀生指的是我们吃的"三净肉"，也就是不是我们亲自杀的，也不是专门为我们杀的。直接杀生，就是亲自宰杀牲畜的行为。无论间接杀生还是直接杀生，都是我们恶业的开始，久而久之便形成一种力量。这种无形的力量牵引着我们朝不善之处一天天走着，于是我们的健康状况开始一天天地发生着变化，高血压、高血脂、高胆固醇等身体的病变接踵而至。尽管如此，杀生在人世间是不可能间断的一件事情，今生你吃我的肉，来世我吃你的肉。今生你杀我，来世我杀你，生生世世终不了。

所以，佛在经典中告诉我们"万般皆离去，唯有业随身"。战争的缘起和我们的杀生有关，但许多人都不明白，也不相信！古代圣贤早就告诉我们"欲知世上刀兵劫，但听夜半屠门声"，人天感应，祸福自召。

今天我们面对这样一个人类自己亲手打造出来的"肉欲横流"的世界，我们应该早早地认清杀生这一事实真相！为了我们的身心健康，为了世界的和平，我们尽量不吃或少吃众生肉吧！

Today, one of my subordinates told me that many people are now killing at the table and greedy for food. Yes, this phenomenon can be seen everywhere. Most people today eat mostly on food and have very little vegetarian food. In the face of such an extremely common phenomenon, I think this is due to the karma of all beings.

The so-called karmic power refers to an invisible force formed by people in the process of doing good or bad karma. This kind of power involuntarily leads us to go to good places or to evil places (That is, the good cause, the better result; the evil cause, the bad result).

Meat diet is the evil karma at the cost of killing, which includes indirect killing and direct killing. Indirect killing refers to the "three clean meats" that we eat. That is, we do not commit suicide, nor specifically for us to kill it. Direct killing is the act of personally slaughtering animals. Indirect or direct killing is the beginning of our bad karma, and it will form a kind of power over time. This kind of invisible force leads us to walk toward the bad ones day by day, so our body's health begins to change every day, and the body's pathological changes such as high blood pressure, high cholesterol, and high cholesterol follow. In spite of this, killing is a thing that cannot be interrupted in the human world. In this life you eat my flesh and in the afterlife I eat your flesh. You kill me in this life, I kill you in the afterlife. Retaliation is not the end of injustice.

Therefore, the Buddha told us in the classics that "All things will leave, and only the karma follows." The origin of the war is related to ourkilling, but many people do not understand it and do

not believe it! The ancient sages had already told us that they "would like to know the swordsman robbers in the world and listen to the sound of the slaughter in the middle of the night." Human heaven induction, fortunes or misfortunes are all created by man himself.

Today we are facing with such a world with overflowing of desire for meat created by human beings. We should recognize the truth about the killing as soon as possible! For the sake of our physical and mental health, for the sake of peace in the world, we try not to eat or eat less meat.

38

大学之道
The principle of Da Xue

大学之道，在明明德，在亲民，在止于至善

The principle of the Da Xue is to promote the bright virtue of people;
influencing the people;
it lies in the perfection to the highest virtue

一天，有人问我："大学之道，在明明德，在亲民，在止于至善"，这段话是什么意思？

其实，这段话是儒家代表作《大学》这篇文章的开篇。这里的"大学"，指的是"大人之学"。什么是大人呢？

"大人"乃圣贤之人，是明了宇宙人生真理的人，是具备高等智慧和心灵品质的人，是心灵、智慧、人格成熟到至高境界的人，是无私奉献、拥有天下格局的人。

"明德"，乃日月之合而明也。明什么？明日月之德，明天地之道，明宇宙、天地、自然的运转法则。天地宇宙在运转过程中所呈现的特征、特性也就是日月的特征和特性。

进而"明明德"就是心灵、智慧、人格、品德能成熟到圣人、贤士的境界，也就是"内圣"的境界。这时才能真正做到"亲民"，亲民是向外付出、善行、全身心地服务大众。效法日月之德，天地之道，用实际行动，无休无止地信受奉行，如此善行直至成就一个高度文明的大同世界！从而也成就了大人"内圣外王"的品质地位。

秋言物语

One day, someone asked me: what is the meaning of the following paragraph. "The principle of the Great Virtue is to promote the bright virtue of people; Influencing the people; It lies in the perfection to the highest virtue."

In fact, the passage at the beginning of the article of the *Da Xue* is a representative of the Confucianists. The "Da Xue" here refers to "The principle of the Great Virtue". What is the Great Virtue ?

The "Great Virtue" is a sage, a person who understands the truth of the universe and the life. He is a person with advanced wisdom and spiritual qualities. He is the person whose mind, wisdom, and personality have matured to the highest level. He is a selfless dedication and a person has the pattern of the world.

The "bright virtue" is the combination of the sun and the moon. What is to understand? Understand the virtue of the sun and the moon, understand the truth of the heaven and the earth. Understand the law of operation of the universe, the heaven, the earth and the nature. The features and characteristics of the universe in its operation are also the features and characteristics of the sun and the moon.

In turn, the "bright virtue" means the mind, wisdom, personality, and the virtue can mature into the realm of the saints and the worthy, that is, the realm of "internal Saints". Only at this time can we truly achieve "Influencing the people, closing to the people", that is to pay outward, be kind, and serve the public wholeheartedly. Follow the rules of the sun and the moon, the way of the heaven and the earth, and practice it with endless faith. Such a good deed will lead to a highly civilized world! As a result, they have also achieved the quality status of the Great Virtue "inside the saint outside the king".

39

止于至善与上善若水
Stop only at the best for the virtue of best is like water

水善利万物而不争，处众人之所恶，故几于道

Water is good and beneficial to all things without disputation,
and it bears the evil of all people, so it is less than the Tao

　　继《秋言物语》的"大学之道"之后，有人问我：《大学》中的
"止于至善"和《道德经》中的"上善若水"，是不是同一个境界？

　　要说明这个问题，首先我们要明白"止于至善"的真正含义。
止于至善是通过我们的心念力、行动力、智慧力使我们的生命完全
做出有益社会和大众的具体实践，并在不断的具体实践中打造一个
和谐美好的人间天堂。

　　再看"上善若水"。上善乃高境界的善，这种善的特征、品性和
水一样，"水善利万物而不争，处众人之所恶，故几于道"。水具备
有益万物的功能，却从不居功自傲。天下所有有情众生（一切动物）

和无情众生（一切植物）都离不开水的滋养。天下所有的污垢，水都能把它洗刷干净，但水永远处于低位。这就是水接近于"道"的特征和品性。

在此，我还想说明的是，水"故几于道"就是接近于道而不完全是道。因为水是有名、有相的，而"道"是无形、无相、无名的。

因此，"止于至善"和"上善若水"是同一境界而不同名的一种说法，都是接近于"道"而不完全是"道"。"道"乃空性，涵养万物而无善恶之分别。"至善"和"上善"还有善恶之分别，而"道"则无善恶之分别，容纳一切。

After the section of "The Principle of Da Xue" of *Qiu's Rhetoric*, someone asked me: Is "up to the best" in *Da Xue* and "the best is like the water" in the *Tao Te Ching* are at the same realm?

To illustrate this issue, we must first understand the true meaning of "up to the best". "Up to the best" is the result of our minds, actions, and wisdom that enable our lives to fully realize the specific practices for the interests of society and the masses, and to create a harmonious and beautiful paradise on the earth with our constant concrete practice.

Look again at "the best is just like the water". The best is the goodness of the high realm. The character and quality of the good are just like the water. "Water is good and beneficial to all things without disputation, and it bears the evil of all people, so it is less than the Tao." Water has the function of benefiting all things, but never proud of itself. All sentient beings (all animals) and ruthless beings (all plants) in the world are inseparable from the nourishment of water. All the dirt in the world, the water can wash it clean, but the water is always low. This is the characteristic and quality of water close to "Tao".

Here, I would also like to explain that water is closely Tao; it is close to Tao but not entirely Tao. Because water has name with phases, but "Tao" is intangible, without phase, without name.

Therefore, the notions of "up to the best" and "the best is just like water" are in the same realm with different names. They are all close to "Tao" and not entirely "Tao". "Tao" is empty, but it contains all things without distinction between good and evil. There is still a difference between good and evil in "up to the best" and "the best is just like water". The "Tao" has no difference between good and evil and accommodates everything.

秋言物语

40

怎样对待错误
How to treat mistakes

行有不得，反求诸己
If you do something wrong, you should find out your
own reasons and review your own mistakes

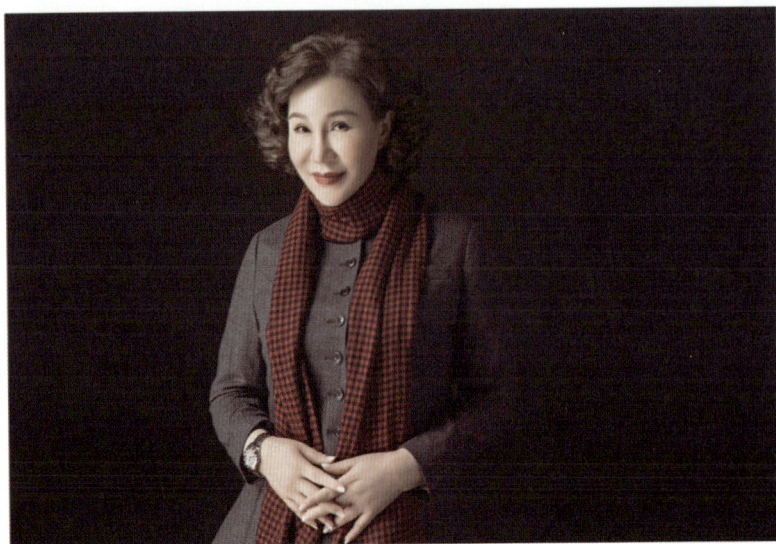

秋言物语

在漫长而又短暂的人生旅途中，我们每一个人都不可避免地犯各种各样的错误。犯错是人生的必然经历。

我们每一个人，从脱胎落地来到这个世界的那一刻开始，我们对自己"为什么来、来做什么，以及我们将要去到哪里"都全然不知。正因为如此，我们才要在自己犯下的错误中，尝识苦果而从中得以清醒。既然人生避免不了犯错，那我们应该怎样对待错误的发生呢？

子贡有曰："君子之过也，如日月之食焉。过也，人皆见之；更也，人皆仰之。"是的，君子的错误，就像太阳和月亮暂时被黑云遮蔽了。过错时人人都看得见，君子一旦承认错误并忏悔、改正了错误，这时人们就像看太阳和月亮一样地仰望君子的光亮。因为君子的本质和品性是优秀的，善根福德是其本来具备的，只是一时的妄想、分别、执着让君子暂时脱离本性而迷失了。

古人云："行有不得，反求诸己。"一个集体的人犯了错，同样也折射出我们自己的错。因此，面对错误，我们每一个人都要深刻地反省自己。

In the long and short life journey, each of us inevitably commits various mistakes. Making mistakes is an indispensable and inevitable experience in life.

Every one of us, from the moment we came to the world from our birth, we are completely unaware of our own "Why come? What we do? Where we are going?" It is precisely because of this that we are to wake up from the mistakes we have made and taste the bitterness. Since life can't avoid mistakes, how should we deal with mistakes?

Zi Gong had a saying, "A gentleman's fault is just like a solar or lunar eclipse: when there is a fault, everyone can see it; when the correction is made, everyone respects it." Yes, a gentleman's mistake, as the sun and moon are temporarily covered by the dark cloud. Everyone can see the fault. Once the gentleman admits his mistake and repents and corrects his mistake, people will respect the gentleman's light like the sun and moon. Because the essence and character of a gentleman are excellent, its good root virtue is originally possessed, but it is only a momentary delusion, separation, and persistence that let the gentleman temporarily get away from his nature and get lost.

The ancients said: "If you do something wrong, you should find out your own reasons and review your own mistakes." When a person in the group makes a mistake, it also reflects our own fault. Therefore, in the face of mistakes, every one of us must deeply introspect ourselves.

41

现在决定未来
The present determines the future

人若好善，福虽未至，其祸已远离；人若好恶，祸虽未至，其福已远离

If a man is good, even though his blessings have not yet come,
his disaster has been far away from him;
if a person like to do evil things, although the disaster has not reach,
his good fortune is far from him

有人问我，那些影、视、歌星们为什么有那么大的福报？有那么多的媒体报道？有那么多的粉丝追捧？同时还拥有那么多金钱与物质？他们的名声远远大过了那些为国家和民族做出重大贡献的科学家、医学家、军事家……这是为什么？

中国有句古语这样讲道："人若好善，福虽未至，其祸已远离；人若好恶，祸虽未至，其福已远离。"影、视、歌星们之所以名利双收，一方面是他们今生的努力拼搏，但另一方面更是他们前世修来的"上天福报"，比如前世乐善好施，用金钱和物质帮助了许多人。今生这些喜爱和追捧他们的人，自然是来报恩的。所以任何事物的得失都是我们自己造就的，现在决定未来。

当然，如果今天大红大紫的明星们不明真相，不懂得珍惜他们的福报因缘，不注重品德和行为的修养，不行善积德回报社会，来世或者今生同样会遭遇不好的结果。

因此，我们不用去羡慕明星们所拥有的名和利，也不要盲目地追捧，他们所拥有的一切，都是他们自己造就的成果。这就是道法自然，这就是因果循环。

Someone asked me, why do the film, TV and pop stars have such a big fortune? Why are there so much media coverage? At the same time they also have so much money and material? Their reputation is far greater than that of scientists, medical scientists, and military strategists who have made great contributions to the country and the nation. Why is that?

There is an ancient Chinese saying: "If a man is good, even though his blessings have not yet come, his disaster has been far away from him; if a person like to do evil things, although the disaster has not reach, his good fortune is far from him." The reason why the stars of movie, video, and singers, have gained the fame and fortune is: on the one hand their efforts in this life, but on the other hand, they have blessing for their practice of their past lives, such as the past life, they were kind and had helped many people with money and material resources. In this life, these people who love and seek after them naturally come to repay the favor. So we make the gains and losses of everything by ourselves, and our present behaviors decide our future fortune.

Of course, if today's big stars do not know the truth, do not know how to cherish their welfare, do not pay attention to the cultivation of morality and behavior, can not be a good return to society, the afterlife or this life will also suffer bad results.

Therefore, we do not have to envy the stars who have the name and profits, nor blindly pursue them. They have everything, that is their own creation. This is the law of the nature, this is the cause and effect circulation.

42

选择大于努力
Choice is greater than efforts

我认为选择，其一需要智慧力，其二需要功德力，其三需要福报力
I think the choice needs first is intellectural power,
second is merit power, third is blessing power

在微信朋友圈里常常看见这样一句话："选择大于努力。"我认为这句话很有道理。一个正确的选择，是走向成功的必然因素。但是怎样才能真正地做出正确的选择，这才是问题的关键所在。

每个人都会面临很多选择，如考学、择业、恋爱、成家等等。然而在现实生活中，我们常常经历十有八九不尽如人意的事情，我们的选择时常出现意想不到的好的或者是不好的结果。这是为什么呢?

我认为选择，其一需要智慧力。无我、利他是一种智慧，这一点说之容易做之难，许多人在"我执""我见"升起之后就全然不顾及别人的感受和利益，这时的私欲和膨胀欲，为自己今后的道路又设置了重重障碍，但当事人全然不知，这就是"所知障"的必然结果。用利他的方式而获得他人的信任和拥护才是智慧的选择。其二，需要功德力。专一、守信是建立功德力最起码的道德标准，一个破坏了自身信誉的人是根本没有立足之地的。其三，需要福报力。乐善好施，助人为乐，凡事都为别人着想，这是获得福报力最为有效的方法。

我们当下所承受的不好的结果，都是我们起心动念所造成的；我们所拥有的好的回报，都是我们当下正确的所思、所想、所行而获得的。

In WeChat's circle of friends, I often see this sentence: "Selection is greater than efforts." I think this sentence is very reasonable. One correct choice is an inevitable factor in the direction of success. But how to make the right choices is the key to the problem.

Everyone faces many choices, such as school, career, love, family, and so on. However, in real life, we often experience things that are not likely to be satisfactory. Our choices often have unexpected good or bad results. Why is this?

I think intellectual power proceeds choice. Selishness, altruism are a kind of wisdom. And this is easy to say, but difficult to do. Many people do not take into account the feelings and interests of others after the "paranoia" and "own opinion" rise. At this time, their desires and inflated desires set up the obstacles for his future road, but they themselves are completely unaware of these. This is the inevitable result of the "knowledge barrier". To gain the trust and support of others in an altruistic way is the choice of wisdom. Second, it requires merit. Specificity and trustworthiness are the minimum moral standards for the establishment of merit, and a person who has undermined his own credibility has no place to live at all. Third, it needs blessing efforts. To be charitable, to help others, and to think of others for all things is the most effective way to obtain good fortune.

The bad results that we suffer now are the results of our mind and thoughts; the good things we have got in return are what we correctly think, consider, and do right now.

43

丁龙的故事
The story of Ding Long

自然本无字，哪有字可识。识字注字意，何解慎深理

There's no word to read. know the word,
note the meaning of the word,
how to understand its very profound reason

在微信朋友圈里，看到了一篇感人至深的有关人物介绍的文章。文章介绍的是一位平凡而伟大的中国人丁龙，一个既不识字又没什么技能的中国人。一百多年前，丁龙为谋生而被贩卖到美国做劳工，成为美国大名鼎鼎的卡朋蒂埃将军的家仆。

卡朋蒂埃将军虽然声名显赫，但沾染了一身不良的习气，视财如命、脾气暴躁，酗酒后会粗暴地打骂仆人。面对这样一个声名显赫却又严重缺乏自身修养的不良之人，所有仆人都选择了离开。但这时的丁龙，以他的忠义之心，说出了最令人动容的语言："虽然你确实脾气很坏，但我认为你毕竟还是个好人，中国的孔夫子曾说过，受人之托，忠人之事。"人要忠心，这就是丁龙之所以没有选择离开的原因。这种智慧的选择，源于其父亲的言传身教。由此可见，家教是何等的重要。

丁龙的父亲，虽然穷到了无力抚养孩子的地步，但他受祖上的教育，把最为重要的人生智慧传给了儿子，以至于丁龙受用一生并成就了平凡而伟大的人生。丁龙能在被贩卖的过程中跟卡朋蒂埃将军结缘，这又何尝不是其祖上的功德所致呢？

丁龙以他的忠义和善良无私的品德，感动并改变了卡朋蒂埃将军，使其最终推动并成就了闻名世界的哥伦比亚大学东亚系（汉学系）的创建与发展。

最后我要说，丁龙的名字跟任何宗教无关，虽然目不识丁，他的智慧、他的忠义来源于祖上的教育。真理无关信仰，更无关宗教。真理的存在即事物本来的实相。任何盲从的宗教，都不及当下的起心动念来得真实。道法自然，自然本无字，哪有字可识，识字注字意，何解慎深理。

In WeChat's friends circle, I read an article with a touching introduction. The article introduces an ordinary and great Chinese Ding Long, a Chinese who was neither literate nor skilled. More than 100 years ago, Ding Long was forced to be sold to the United States as a laborer for living and became a household servant of the famous American General Carpentier.

Although General Carpentier was famous, he was tangled with bad habits, took money as his life with a quick temper, and he would brutally beat his servants after drinking. In the face of such a bad person who was notorious but lacking of self-cultivation, so that all his servants chose to leave. At this time, Ding Long, with his loyalty, said the most moving language: Although he is really bad tempered, but I think he is still a good person after all. Chinese Confucius once said,

66 To be trusted, to be loyal, to be faithful." This is why Ding Long did not choose to leave. The choice of wisdom stemmed from his father's words and deeds. This shows how important tutorship is.

Ding Long's father was poor. Although he was too poor to raise his children, he was educated by his ancestors and passed on his most important life wisdom to his son. So that Ding Long had spent it his entire life and had achieved an extraordinary and great life. Ding Long could be associated with General Carpentier in the process of being sold. Is this not the result of his ancestral virtues?

Ding Long touched and changed General Carpentier with his loyalty, goodness and selfless devotion, which ultimately promoted and accomplished the establishment and development of the world-famous East Asian Department of Chinese Studies (Department of Sinology) at Columbia University.

In the end, I would like to say that Ding Long's name has nothing to do with any religion. His wisdom and loyalty come from the inliterate words and deeds of the previous generation. Truth has nothing to do with faith, and has nothing to do with religion. The existence of truth is the actual reality of things. No religion that blindly follows is as real as the current motivation. Tao is the nature. The nature is nothing. There is no word in nature. There's no word to read. Know the word, note the meaning of the word, how to understand its very profound reason.

44

无人超市带来的思考
Reflections on an unattended supermarket

人法地，地法天，天法道，道法自然
Man acts after the earth, the earth after the heaven,
the heaven after the Tao, and the Tao after the nature

看到一则新闻报导，说马云的无人超市在杭州开业了。这在很多人看来，无疑又是一项高科技成果，但我个人对此事的看法并不乐观。

表面看来，无人超市节省了大量的人力、物力，但这仅仅是商家的利益。从国家乃至整个人类的层面来看，它的出现未必是一件好事。大量的"无人化"取代了"有人化"的操作，将造成大量的人员失业，而失业人员的增加，必将给国家和社会造成严重的负担。我们尚没有足够的社会保障能力，我们拿什么来保证这些失业人员的生存和生活问题？与此同时，我们又有什么样的措施和方法，来维持社会的安定团结？这难道不是一个令人十分担心的问题吗？

中华民族五千多年以来，祖先为我们留下了无数文化遗产和科

技发明：指南针、造纸术、印刷术、火药乃至中医等。古人的这些发明创造无一不是遵道而行："人法地，地法天，天法道，道法自然。"人法地——厚德载物，地法天——天道酬勤，天法道——天是道的产物。道生万物而本自自然。

高科技的发展给人类带来大量便利的同时，也在不知不觉中使人类丧失了本来具有的行为能力。没有基本的劳作，一切都来得那么容易，将来的人类从外形到智能将是一个怎样的状况？

据史料记载，上古的人类具备千里眼、顺风耳，但今天有人相信吗？完全不可能相信！我们只会认为那是神话，那是人们想象出来的。但通过目前的社会现象看，试想一下，随着科技的发展，我们完全可以饭来张口、衣来伸手，一切都可以坐享其成，四体不勤，五谷不分。到那时，我们将在丧失功能的同时丧失掉我们几千年的文化。

当今，科学技术推动人类进步是必然趋势，但怎样合理化、有序化地加以应用，才是我们防微杜渐、防患于未然的关键所在。

I read a news report saying that Ma Yun's unattended supermarket opened in Hangzhou. This is undoubtedly a high-tech achievement in the eyes of many people, but my personal opinion on this matter is not so optimistic.

On the surface, unattended supermarkets save a lot of manpower and material resources, but this is only the interests of businesses. Judging from the perspective of the country and even the entire human population, its appearance is not necessarily a good thing. When a large amount of "unmanned" replaces the "humanization" operation, a large number of unemployed people will be created, and the increase in unemployed people will inevitably impose a serious burden on the country and society. We do not have enough social security capabilities. What are we going to do to ensure the survival and livelihood of the unemployed? At the same time, what kind of measures and methods do we have to maintain social stability and unity? Isn't this a very worrying issue?

The Chinese nation has a history of more than 5,000 years, since then, our ancestors have left us with countless cultural heritage and technological inventions: compasses, papermaking, printing, gunpowder, and even Chinese medicine. The inventions and creations of the ancients were all in accordance with the principle of Tao: "Man acts after the earth, the earth after the heaven, the heaven after the Tao, and the Tao after the nature." Man acts after the earth — great virtue bears great wealth; the earth after the heaven — God rewards the diligent; the heaven after the Tao — the heaven is the product of the Tao. Tao is born of all things, but it is born of the nature.

While the development of the high technology has brought a lot of convenience to the mankind, the human beings have also lost their original abilities to perform without knowing it. It is easy to get everything without basic labor. What kind of situation of the mankind will look like in the future from their external shape to their intelligence?

According to the records of the ancient history, we have ancient people with clairvoyant eyes and ears, but today is there someone believe it? It is impossible to believe! We can only think of it as a myth. It is what the people think of. However, judging from the current social phenomenon, imagine that with the development of science and technology, we can completely open our mouths with food, reach out our hands with clothes, and everything can be enjoyed. Can neither do physical work nor distinguish rice from wheat. By then, we will lose our culture for thousands of years while losing our functions.

Today, science and technology are an inevitable trend to promote human progress. However, how rationalization, ordering, and scientific application are the keys to our preventing before it happens.

45

关于企业管理
On corporate management

同样是一群人，一个办公场所，却演绎着不一样的企业故事

They are the same group of people and one office,
but they make different stories of the company

昨天在和朋友谈到关于企业管理的话题时，朋友认为鼎益丰的成功在很大程度上取决于企业文化。对朋友的这一看法，我表示认同。

　　何为企业？在我看来很简单：一群人，一个办公场所，具备相应的合法手续，就构成了一家企业。但每家企业的形式和内核各不相同，鼎益丰是精神和物质的结合体。同样是一群人，一个办公场所，却演绎着不一样的企业故事。

　　早晨的五声鼓响、五声钟鸣后，开始了《道德经》的诵读。朗朗的诵读经声，传递着千年的文化，散发着圣贤的智慧，振奋着民族的精神！这是鼎益丰七年来风雨无阻的晨会。

　　晨会制是我创办鼎益丰的纲领，许多人赞叹鼎益丰坚持七年而纲领未改，而在我的感受中从未有过"坚持"。它仅仅是一种自然而然的事，自然得就像吃早餐一样。

　　我认为成功的企业管理取决于企业的文化建设、核心技术和人才培养。文化建设是提升员工人生观、价值观、道德观的重要组成部分。核心技术是保证企业经济效益不可缺少的根本要素和命脉。它在很大程度上是不可复制的，并且具备在相当长时间内的不可超越性。企业最得心应手的人才，都是在企业自身的土壤里成长起来的，完全是根据企业发展的需求，而培养的德才兼备的人才。这里除了企业文化的打造之外，还需要逐步建立健全一套教育体系，以适应企业，乃至国家和民族利益的需要。这是培养人才的责任心、使命感和胸怀天下的大格局。

因此，企业管理没有完全固定的模式，同时也没有一成不变的方法，它是随着企业不断发展而变化的。但它自始至终都贯穿着企业创始人的思想和理念，这是企业发展永远不变的根本。

Yesterday, I talked with friends about the topic of corporate management. My friends thought that the success of Ding Yifeng depends on its corporate culture to a large extent. I agree with this view of the friends.

What is a business? In my opinion, it is very simple: a group of people, an office, and the corresponding legal procedures constitute a company. However, each company's form and core are different. Ding Yifeng is a combination of spirit and material. It is also a group of people, an office space, but it makes a different company story.

In the morning, at five drums and five bells, the reading of *Taoism* starts. The reading sounds spread the culture of the millennium, exude the wisdom of the sages, and inspire the spirit of the nation! This is the morning meeting of Ding Yifeng constaint for 7 years rain or shine.

The morning meeting system is my program to establish Ding Yifeng. Many people praised that Ding Yifeng has insisted on for 7 years, but the program has not been changed, and I have no "insisting" in my feelings. It's just a natural thing. It's just like having breakfast.

I believe that the successful corporate management depends on the company's cultural development, its core technologies, and the talent cultivation. The cultural construction is an important part

of improving employees' outlook on life, values, and ethics. The Core technology is the essential element and lifeline to ensure the economic growth of an enterprise. It is largely non-reproducible and has an unsurpassed ability for quite a long time. The cultivation of talents: The most talented people in the company are all grown up in the soil of the company itself. It is based solely on the needs of the company's development to cultivate the staff of both moral and intellectual abilities. Apart from building corporate culture, it is also necessary to gradually establish and improve a complete education system to meet the needs of enterprises and even the interests of the country and the nation. This is a big pattern of cultivating talents with a sense of responsibility, mission, and mind.

Therefore, corporate management does not have a completely fixed model. At the same time, it does not have a static method. It is constantly changing methods as companies continue to develop. But at the same time, it always runs through the thoughts and concepts of the founders of the company. It's the very essence of business development.

放下小我，成就大我

Put down the ego to achieve the greater self

"小我"自私自利，"大我"无我利他

The "ego" is selfish,
the "greatman" is altruistic

这两天，有一个问题一直盘旋在我的脑海里：怎样才能真正做到放下小我、成就大我？

　　我认为"小我"就是一切以自身利益为出发点的思想和行为。在一个团体里着眼于自我的个人利益，在一个公司里着眼于自己团队的利益，在一个国家里着眼于自己公司的利益，这些都是小我的表现。"大我"就是一切以他人利益为出发点的思想和行为。在团体里个人利益服从团体利益，在公司里团体利益服从公司利益，在国家层面公司利益服从国家利益，这就是一个不断放大自我的过程。无论处在什么样的境地，都能把个人利益放下，一切以他人、团体、公司、国家乃至全人类的利益为目标的大胸怀，才是真正成就"大我"人生的天下格局。一句话："小我"自私自利，"大我"无我利他。

　　例如，有人说，鼎益丰是一家民营企业，将来做得更大有风险怎么办？我认为，所有的风险都来自自私和贪婪。我们从做鼎益丰之初就没想着公司是为自己而做的。鼎益丰能有今天的成就都源于这块土地，这个国家和中国共产党的正确领导，这是不可否认的事实。假如没有这片土地，没有我们的国家，没有我们伟大的党，哪有鼎益丰的存在？没有父母，哪有孩子！所以上报国土恩、国家恩和共产党的恩德才是我们努力的方向！

These two days, a question has been hovering in my mind: how can I really do to put down the ego, to achieve the greater self?

I think the "ego" is all thoughts and actions that take one's own interests as their starting points. It is the performance of the ego to focus on personal interests in a group, to focus on the interests of one's own team in a company, and to focus on the interests of one's own company in a country. All these are the performances of the ego. The "big self" is all thoughts and behaviors that take the interests of others as their starting points. It is a process of constantly enlarging oneself that the individual interests are subordinated to the group interests in the group, the group interests to the company interests in the company, and the corporate interests to the national interests at the national level. No matter what kind of situation you are in, you can put down your personal interests. All the big minds that aim at the interests of others, groups, companies, countries, and even all mankind are the world patterns that truly achieve the "big self" of life. One word: the "ego" is selfish, the "great man" is altruistic.

For example, some people say: Ding Yifeng is a private enterprise. What if there are risks to doing more in the future? I think all the risks come from selfishness and greed. We didn't think the company was built for ourselves from the beginning. It is an undeniable fact that Ding Yifeng's achievements today are due to this land, this country and the correct leadership of the Communist Party of China. Without this land, without our country and without our great Party, where is Ding Yifeng's existence? Without parents, there are no children! That's why we're going to pay a debt of gratitude to our motherland, to our country and to the Communist Party of China! This is the direction of our endeavor.

47

悟为本，修为末
Enlighten first, practice afterward

真理就是宇宙人生
Truth is the reality of
the universe and life

记得儿时唱国际歌的时候，印象最为深刻的是："满腔的热血已经沸腾，要为真理而斗争。"那时候，虽然感觉到"真理"二字很神圣，却不明其意，几十年来我一直在找寻答案。

真理到底是什么，今天终于有些明了：真理就是宇宙人生，或者是万事万物的真实之相，真实之相是永恒不变的，它不会因人、因事、因时而发生任何的改变。所以真理不是谁发明创造的，真理只是人们对它的认知程度不同而已。

真理的另一个代名词就是"道"。人们普遍认为道是修成的。换言之，觉悟真理是修出来的。其实不然，道是悟在先、修在后，没有开悟真理之道。我们如何修行呢？修是明了之后的行为，也叫修为，同时也是悟道前提下的行为。

不悟而修，是盲修，盲修是带着欲望和妄想的修，而恰恰被欲望和妄想所束缚，其结果是"如露亦如电，应作如是观"。悟道之后的修行是天人合一的境界。记得一位觉悟的大师说过一段话，其大意是这样：觉悟前是当局者迷，开悟后是旁观者清；觉悟前是为成功而拼命，开悟后是无事以取天下；觉悟前以局部看局部，以现象看现象，觉悟后以整体看局部，以本质看现象；觉悟前我在矛盾中生活，觉悟后我在圆满中存在，以道立天下，抱一为天下式。

When I remember singing the International Song when I was a child, my most impression was: "The blood is boiling, to fight for truth". "At that time, I felt that the word "truth" was sacred, but I did not understand its meaning. I have been looking for the answers for decades.

What is the truth at the end? It is finally clear today: Truth is the reality of the universe and life, or the true reality of all things. The reality of truth is eternal. It does not change due to a person, an event, or time. Therefore, the truth is not who invented and created. The truth is that the people have awareness of it at different degrees.

Another synonym for truth is "Tao". It is generally believed that Tao was cultivated. In other words, the realization of the truth was cultivated. In actual fact, the Tao is realized first, and practice after. There is no way to enlighten the truth. How do we practice? The practice is the act after understanding, it is also known as cultivation; it is also the act of enlightenment of Tao.

Therefore, practice is changeable, impermanent and promising. At the same time, it is also a constant birth and death. There is no end for the spiritual practice, but the consciousness is only at one conception. Therefore, consciousness is the innateness, and practice is the end of cultivation. The end of the practice cannot be reversed; the consciousness is the body, and cultivation is for use; the body and use are in one. That is the ways of the nature.

To practice without understanding is to practice blindly.Blindly practicing is a practice with desire and delusion. It is precisely bound by desires and delusions. The result is that "Like dew or like electricity, it should be seen that way". The practice after enlightenment is the realm of the unity of the heaven and the man. I remember that a master of enlightenment said such a paragraph, the general idea is this: Before the enlightenment is the superstition of the party; after enlightenment is the bystander who i s clear; before enlightenment is to desperate for success, after enlightenment is nothing that can be taken from the world; before enlightenment is local Look at the local phenomenon, and see the phenomena through phenomena. After awakening, look at the local with a whole view, and see the phenomenon as an essence. Before awakening, I lived incontradictions. Aftermy enlightenment, I existed in my satisfactory, to stand with the Tao, and hold one for the world.

48

生与死
On life and death

爱之欲其生，恶之欲其死
When you love someone, you always want him to keep alive;
When you hate someone, you always want him to die

所谓"爱之欲其生，恶之欲其死"。人从哪里来？人从爱欲中来；人到哪里去？人在恶中死去。

人是爱欲的产物，因为爱欲人类得以不断地繁衍。爱欲是生命的源泉，然而三界十方，生死相续。当人在爱欲中诞生的那一刻，也就意味着死亡的到来。不悟得真理，人永远不知道生命的真谛，人永远不知道怎么摆脱生死，同样人也永远不知道自己因何而生，又因何而死。

说到摆脱生死，绝大部分人不会相信，因为死亡是人类世界的常态，谁也无法抗拒。但了悟真理的智者，能从人类由生到死的常态中找到一条解脱之路，这是何等的境界啊！这种可以突破死亡的方法说出来也许不会有人能信。是的，真理往往掌握在少数人手里。然而，怎样才能真正达到摆脱生死的境界呢？

那就是，勇敢地断除爱的欲望，这里包括爱人、爱物、爱名、爱利等等。人因爱而产生贪欲、嗔恨、愚痴、邪恶、骄傲等五种毒害身体的因素，烦恼、忧苦和悲伤油然而生，于是生、老、病、死如期到来。如此这般，完成了生命由生到死的过程。

我们很难断除爱的欲望，但至少我们要明白人生的真正含义。因为有生死，我们才有了努力的空间；因为有生死，才有更多的可能。唯变所适，学习在于求证。

A saying goes like "We want him/her to be immortal when loving someone, while want him/her to be dead when hating someone". Then, where is man coming from and where is man going to? Man derives from lust and dies in evil.

Man is the outcome of lust, by which man is multiplied. Lust signifies the origin of life. Then, life and death continue after coming through on the world. At the moment man is born from lust, it prophesies the coming of death. Without realizing the life truth, man will never understand the essence of life. And man will never know how to cast off their relations with life and death, and what does he/she live as well as die for.

Most people don't believe on casting off the relationship with life and death, because death is the normal state of the world where human lives and nobody can resist it. However, the wise man who realizes the life truth can achieve moksa in man's normal state from birth to death. What an amazing state! Seldom do people believe on the method in freeing oneself from death. For sure, the truth is usually mastered by few people. So, how can we reach the moksa state?

The way is to break off affectional greed, including the people and things you like, reputation, treasure and etc. Man begins to have the five emotions that may poison his body such as greed, hatred, ignorance, evil, arrogance and the like due to affection, following with annoyance, worries and sorrowfulness, and eventually birth, aging, disease and death are doomed to come forth. In this way does man finish his life from birth to death.

It's hard to remove our greed on what we like, but at least we should understand the real meaning of life. With life and death, we have space to strive for; with life and death, there are more possibilities. Learning lies in proving, so we should adjust ourselves to the right circumstance.

深圳精神
—— 勤与善
Shenzhen Spirit: diligence and goodness

居善地，心善渊；与善仁，言善信
Live in good land, with a good mind,
good benevolence, and good faith

　　昨晚，公司一位刚刚入职的员工，由于家中发生了一件不幸的事，急需几万块钱解燃眉之急，以尽孝道。当我在电话里听到他难于启齿的忐忑和心急如焚的声音时，我即刻放下手中的事，凑了几万块钱通知他来取钱。当他从我手中接过钱的时候，几乎要跪下来，以表感激。我本能地急忙说道："你别这样，赶紧起来。"那一刻，我的眼眶湿润了，雪中送炭，让我的心灵得以安宁。

　　一个小小的善举，让我想起《道德经》中"居善地，心善渊；与善仁，言善信"这句话。深圳是一个蓬勃发展的现代化城市，无论你来自何方，这片土地都能给予你生长和发展的机会。但在此，任何一个有追求的人都需要勤奋，在你追我赶中拼搏奋进。我曾一度感到，来到深圳就像踩上一条火线，你只有不停地向前奔跑，才不至于被脚下的火线烫伤双脚。

　　不知道为什么，此刻，我的脑海里忽然响起了一阵急促的敲打木鱼声。为什么出家的修行人要敲打木鱼呢？因为鱼在水中除了昼夜不停地游动之外，它们从来到这个世上，就不曾合目。这就是修行人为什么要敲打木鱼的原因，昼夜不寐，天道酬勤。

　　懒惰不仅是人生贫穷的根，也是身体百病的源。富贵须养德，健康须勤奋。至今我仍然清楚地记得，十二年前，我刚到深圳时，在大街的广告牌上看到的两句话：一句是"时间就是金钱，效率就是生命"；另一句是"送人玫瑰，手有余香"。这两句话就是深圳这座现代化城市的真正含义——勤奋而善良。

　　勤奋，乃有为之方法，它能给你带来财富，而善良则是无为之举。"送人玫瑰，手有余香"是自然之道，我们不贪求余香，更不贪求回报，这就是为什么当年梁武帝佛心天子，广造佛寺，修整经书，勤劝众人出家，而达摩祖师却说他毫无功德。因为梁武帝的所作所为，皆有贪得回报的心念，所以，这就是后来梁武帝未得善终的原因。

Last night, a newly recruited employee of the company, due to an unfortunate incident at home, urgently needed tens of thousands of RMB Yuan to relieve his urgency and dedicate himself to filial piety. When I heard him on the phone, he was hard to say and rushed voice, I immediately put down what was in my hands and collected tens of thousands of Yuan and asked him to come to take the money. When he took the money from me, he almost crouched down to express his gratitude. I spontaneously hurriedly said, "Don't do this, hurry up". At that moment, my eyes were moist, and I lost in thinking to offer coal in snowy weather to solve the urgent needs of others, letting my mind be at peace.

A small charity reminds me of the words: "Live in good land, with a good mind, good benevolence, and good faith" in *Tao Te Ching*. Shenzhen is a booming and modern city. No matter where you come from, this land can give you opportunities for growth and development. But here, any person with ambition needs to be diligent. All need to fight and forge ahead as you chase me. I once felt that when I came to Shenzhen, it was like stepping on a hot line. You only have to keep running forward so that your feet will not be burnt by the line of fire under your feet.

Do not know why, at this moment, my mind suddenly sounded a sudden sound of knocking wooden fish. Why would a monk knock on a wooden fish? Because the fish swims in the water, day and night, its eyes never come to close since it comes to the world.

This is why the practitioners must beat the wooden fish. They stay up late day and night, and heaven rewards.

Laziness is not only the root of poverty in life, but also the source of all diseases. Wealth requires virtue, and health requires diligence. So far I still clearly remember that when I first arrived in Shenzhen 12 years ago, I saw two sentences on the billboard on the street: "Time is money, efficiency is life" and "Give roses to other, fragrance left on your hands". These two sentences are the real meaning of this modern city in Shenzhen- diligent and goodness.

Diligence is a way to success. It can bring wealth to you; and kindness is an act of inaction. "Give roses to other, fragrance left on your hands" that is to say: helping others makes one happier. This is the natural way. We do not seek aftertaste, let alone reward. This is why Liang Wudi, the Emperor with the Buddha's mind, built a lot of Buddhist temples, repaired the scriptures, and often advised everyone to become a monk, but Dharma Patriarch said that he had no merit. Because of what Liang Wudi did, there was a greedy, rewarding mind. Therefore, this was the reason why Liang Wudi had no good end.

50 ——————————————————

心念的结果
The result of mind

长短相形，高下相倾，音声相和，前后相随
Long and short, high and low, sound and voice,
before and after were born against each other

    其实，我们每个人成长的过程都是一张 K 线图，或在起伏中上升，或在起伏中下降。同样，一家企业的发展也是如此。上升是善因的果，下降是恶因的缘。无论是上升，还是下降，都是一种修炼。明理者当知"长短相形，高下相倾，音声相和，前后相随"之理，这就是事物发展变化的必然规律，这就是事物本来的真实之相。

    我们每人都希望生命健康长寿，我们每天都祝愿企业一帆风顺，但现实中，往往有许多不如人意的事，于是烦恼油然而生，怨气由此而来，殊不知上升下降都是心念的结果。

    世上本无事，庸人自扰之。凡事都由心所生，60% 的疾病受心情影响。用情生烦恼，忘念转正心，天堂地狱即在当下。所谓通

过努力我们可以去到那美丽的天堂，其实那个美丽的天堂即在当下。心平静了、宽广了、慈悲善良了，即喜、即乐、即天堂；嗔恨了、烦恼了、痛苦了，甚至疾病了，即苦、即痛、即地狱。

Actually, each of us grows up as a K-line map, or it rises in ups and downs, or goes down in the ups and downs. Similarly, the development of a company is also the same. Rising is the fruit of good causes, and decline is the cause of evil causes. Whether it is rising or falling is a kind of cultivation. A reasonable person should know the principle of "long and short, high and low, sound and voice, before and after were born against each other". It is the inevitable law of the development and change of things; that is, the true nature of things.

Every day we want to live a long and healthy life. Every day we wish our company is going smoothly. However, in reality, many things are often unsatisfactory. Therefore, our troubles arise out of nothing. Our grievances come from this. We do not know that rising and falling are all mind results.

There is nothing in the world, mediocre person self-interference. All things are born of mind, and 60% of the diseases are caused by one's mood. To create trouble with emotion, the delusion turns the right mind.

The heaven and hell are at the present moment. We can go to that beautiful paradise through hard work. In fact, that beautiful paradise is in the moment. When mind is calm, broad, compassionate and kind, that is, joy, that is, happiness, that is, heaven; the moment hated, annoyed, painful, even sick, that is, bitter, pain, that is, hell.

51

好女人是一所学校、一本书
A good woman is a school, a book

好女人是一所学校，好女人是一本书
A good woman is a school and the good woman is a book

　　这两天，当儿时的玩伴、青年时的闺蜜出现在跟前的时候，许多青春往事又再现在记忆的屏幕上，画面清晰而透彻。

闺蜜和我同校不同班，但我们极为相似的是文科好、理科差。数、理、化，从心往外排斥的东西，自然是学不好，于是轮到工资升级考试时，面对考卷我们都失败了，几个题都出错或不会做。考卷交回给老师后，我俩商议怎么办，于是一个不良的行为发生了：

两个不到 20 岁的小女孩，趁着夜色，跑到车间，用锯片打开了车间工程师办公室的门，考卷就在工程师的抽屉里。我在门外放哨，她把考卷拿出来，翻出我俩的考卷，急忙纠正和填答案，再把考卷放回去。为了不露痕迹，她还把两颗老鼠屎放在考卷上，这意味着考卷未曾动过，即使老师发现动了，那也是老鼠的事，就这样我们通过了考试。

与此同时，我们又都是热爱文学的青年，她的文笔很好，当年的文章还上过《铁道报》，而我更侧重哲学方面的研究。

当年在杂志上看到这样两句话：好女人是一所学校，好女人是一本书。当时对这两句话的理解虽然不像现在这样深刻，但内心里非常想做一所学校、一本书。

如今，几十年过去了，当年的起心动念，让我的人生在千锤百炼中成长，在风雨雷电中铸就，在失败与成功中不断地书写和建造。如今，雪染双鬓，初心未改——好女人是一所学校，好女人是一本书。

In these two days, when childhood playmate and young friend appeared in front of my eyes, many youth memories are now on the screen of my memory. The pictures are clear and thorough.

The girlfriends were in different classes at the same school, but we were very similar good in arts and bad in science. Mathematics, physics, chemistry were excluded from the mind, they were naturally not good, but when it comes to the salary upgrade exam, we were all lost in the face of examination papers. Some questions were wrong or not done. When the examination papers were handed back to the teacher, we discussed what to do and a bad behavior happened:

Two little girls less than 20 years old, taking advantage of the night, went to the workshop and opened the door of the workshop engineer's office with a saw blade. The examination papers were in the engineer's drawer. I watched the whistle outside the door. She took out the test papers, pulled out our examination papers, hurriedly corrected and filled in the answers, and put the test papers back. In order not to show signs, she also placed two mice shits on the examination papers. This meant that the examination paper had not been touched. Even if the teacher found out that it was a matter of the mouse, we passed the examination.

At the same time, we were all young people who loved literature. Her writing style was very good. Her articles were published on the *Railway News* that year, and I focused more on philosophical research.

In the magazine that year I saw two sentences: a good woman is a school, a good woman is a book. Although the understanding of these two sentences at the time was not as profound as it is now, I really wanted to be a school or a book from within.

Now, decades have passed, my dream made my life grown up through a thousand trials and tribulations, forged in storms and lightning, and written and constructed in failure and success. Today, the snow has stained the double temples, but the mind has not changed at the beginning: a good woman is a school and the good woman is a book.

52

受苦消苦，离苦得乐

Suffering reduces sufferings,
no pain comes from happiness

人总是在得失中欢乐着、痛苦着，
这就是人世间一阴一阳的人之常道

People are always joyful and painful in their gains and losses.
This is the normal course of a person in the world of Yin and Yang

常言道："人生苦短。"这句话不难理解，意思是说，人生是痛苦
而短暂的。纵观大千世界，芸芸众生，有多少人痛苦，又有多少人
欢乐呢？通过现象我们可以看到人生苦乐各占一半。

人生的痛苦都来自内心深处放不下自己的得失，痛苦皆因自己
所求不能如愿，或者是得到之后的失去。正如老子所言"不知常，
妄作凶"，不知道事物的规律而乱思乱行，就产生了不好的结果，痛
苦随之而产生。由于无知而乱做，我们自己制造了痛苦，当然要由
我们自己来承受。人总在得失中欢乐着、痛苦着，这就是人世间一
阴一阳的人之常道。

　　那么人生有没有少苦多乐，或常常欢乐的状态呢？其实是有的，只是我们不知道什么方法才能使我们远离痛苦而常常欢乐。

　　佛学中有句话讲到了事物的真相，那就是"受苦消苦，享福消

福"，这说明人在受苦的时候，正处在消除痛苦的过程中，精神的痛苦或肉体的痛苦都是如此。因此当痛苦向我们袭来的时候，我们以接纳和欢喜的心态来对待，这时痛苦就随之而变成欢乐，苦去方能甘来。

As the saying goes: "Life is painful and short." This sentence is not difficult to understand. It means that life is painful and short-lived. Looking at the world, all living beings, how many people are suffering and how many people are happy? From the phenomenon we can see that life is half-bitter and half sweet.

The pain of life comes from the depths of the mind that can't let go of one's own gains and losses, and the pain is due to one's desire not to be able to do so, or to be lost afterwards. As Lao Zhu said, "The frivolous behaviors that do not recognize the natural laws often cause troubles and disasters." If we don't know the laws of things and think about things indiscriminately, we got bad results, and the pain rises. Because of ignorance and chaos, we create our own pain, and of course we must bear it. People are always joyful and painful in their gains and losses. This is the normal course of a person in the world of Yin and Yang.

Does life have less bitterness and more joy, or is it often a state of joy? Actually there are, but we do not know what methods can make us often joy away from suffering.

There is a saying in Buddhism that tells the truth of things, that is, "To suffer is to remove one's sufferings, and to enjoy happiness is to remove one's blessing." This shows that when people suffer, they are in the process of eliminating suffering, whether it is spiritual pain or physical pain. That's it. So when pain comes to us, we treat it with an attitude of acceptance and rejoicing. At this time, the pain will turn into joy, and when the pain is gone and the good luck will come.

53

企业管理的虚实之道
The virtual and practical way of corporate management

以爱心、信心、决心、打造健康生命，铸就非凡企业

Build a healthy life with love, confidence and determination,
and create extraordinary enterprises

血肉筋骨构成了人的身体，五脏六腑通过经络而相互连接。何为经络？对人体生命而言，经络是看不见、摸不着，但又起着决定性作用的、非物质性的、实际存在的东西。经络如同一个城市的交通图，经为主干道，络为主干所延伸出的许多条支干道，所以人体经络如同网络一般，在人体中自然而有序地运行着。因此，人体整个构造的本身就是一虚一实、一阴一阳，虚实相应、阴阳相合，构成我们完整的生命体。

世间万物本相通。有人问我企业管理的经验，我认为企业的管理如同人体的健康管理，是"此两者，同出而异名"的关系。

常言道："麻雀虽小，五脏俱全。"企业的创始人和高层管理者是经，而基层的员工是络，企业的文化是魂魄，企业的各个部门是五脏六腑，而企业运营的各个项目是血肉筋骨。企业的生命体和人的命体是相同的，它是一件同理不同体的事。

所以如果没有参悟宇宙人生的真谛，我们会带着错误的知见而妄为，妄为的后果使我们把自己折磨得死去活来。"高者下为基"，企业之所以成功，那是因为有员工作为基础，手心手背都是肉，胳膊和腿缺一不可，牵一发而动全身。因此老板对于企业各部门以及所有员工都不能分别对待，更不能上下对立，左右不顾，应当视同仁如亲人，以爱心、信心、决心，打造健康生命，铸就非凡企业。

The blood, flesh, tendons and bones form the human body, and the five viscera and six puffs are connected inside and outside with the meridians. What is the meridians? For human life, meridians and collaterals are invisible and intangible, but they play a decisive role non-material and practical. The meridian is like a traffic map of a city. The meridian is a trunk road that connects many branch roads. Therefore, the meridian of the human body is like a network, and it runs automatically and orderly in the human body. Therefore, the entire structure of the human body itself is a virtual reality, a Yin and a Yang, virtual and practical, and a combination of Yin and Yang, which constitutes our complete living body.

All things in the world are connected. Someone asked me the experience of enterprise management. I think that the management of a company is like the management of human health. It is the relationship between the two, "both, with the same source and different names".

As the saying goes: "The sparrow is small, but it has fully internal organs," the founder and senior manager of the company are the business leaders just like meridians, and the employees at the grassroots level are the partners just like collaterals. The culture of the company is the soul; the various departments of the company are the internal organs of the five viscera and six puffs and the enterprises operate various projects. It is bloody flesh bones. The enterprise's life and human's life are the same. It is a matter with the same reason but in different bodies.

Therefore, if we do not understand the truth of the universe, we will want only act with the wrong ideas. The consequences of turmoil make us torture ourselves to death. The "higher ones take the lowers as the foundations". The reason why companies succeed is because there are employees as the foundation, and the hand palms and backs are all flesh and meat. Arms and legs are indispensable, one links the whole body. Therefore, the boss can not be separate and

persistent from all departments of the company and all employees. Even more can not up and down, left and right. They should treat as their loved ones and build a healthy life with love, confidence and determination, and create extraordinary enterprises.

54

企业的用人之道
HR and employment

善良、包容、爱心、耐心、决心，是培养人才的摇篮
Kindness, tolerance, love, patience,
and determination are the cradle of talent

作为企业的领导者，我曾常常感叹德才兼备的人才太少。但有一天当我静下心来仔细思考时，才发现不是人才少，而是领导者的包容和善良程度不够，才会造成人才的缺失。

就企业而言，我们本身就需要各种不同类型的人才。一水润万物，而万物生长则各不相同。人人都有其个别差异，在用人之道上，我认为不必完全求同，只需大同小异。领导者必须身先士卒，用自己的行为和品德去化育人才，而不是用高压方式去管理人才。善良、包容、爱心、耐心和决心是培养人才的摇篮。我们维护企业秩序的良好方法应该是求同存异、彼此包容、相互尊重，从而保持

　　和而不同，调动每个人的主观能动性，使其发挥最大作用，为企业发展做出贡献。

　　不同类型、各有所长的人才会聚，是构成企业人才架构的基本元素。因此我们共同的事情只有一件，那就是品德修养。只要品德修养相同，其他任何的生活方式、行为习惯、专业技能则不必相同。企业的整体思维告诉我们，人与人都是相互依存、无法独立的。我们只有携起手来以和合的仁义情怀来化解矛盾和冲突，共同完成道德修养的落实，才可以彼此实现人生的价值。

As a corporate leader, I have often lamented that there are too few talented individuals. But one day when I calmed down and thought carefully, I discovered that not a few talented people, but a leader's tolerance and kindness were not enough to cause the loss of talent.

As far as company is concerned, we ourselves need various types of talents. The rain breeds all things, and all things grow differently. Everyone has its own individual differences. In the way of employing people, I don't think it is necessary to completely seek common ground. It only needs to be very similar. Leaders must take the lead and use their own behaviors and morals to educate their talents instead of using high-pressure methods to manage them. Kindness, tolerance, love, patience, and determination are the cradle of talent. Our good approach to maintaining corporate order should be to seek common ground while reserving differences, tolerate each other and respect each other, so as to maintain harmony but to mobilize each person's subjective initiative, to play its greatest role, and to contribute to the development of the enterprise.

The convergence of talents of different types and talents of enterprises constitutes the basic elements of the corporate talent structure. Therefore, there is only one thing we share, that is moral cultivation. As long as moral cultivation is the same, other lifestyles, behaviors, and professional skills do not have to be the same. The overall thinking of the company tells us that people and people are interdependent and cannot be independent. Only when we join hands to resolve conflicts and conflicts through harmony and benevolence, can we complete the accomplishment of moral accomplishment before we can achieve each other's values in life.

55

生命的道法自然
Life follows nature

风起的时候在空中潇洒自如，
风止的时候在地上随遇而安，这就是自在随缘
when the wind rises, it will flow freely in the air.
When the wind stops, it will be on the ground. It is free and easy

　　国庆、中秋难得的双节假期，我来到了英国伦敦。经过一个小时左右的车程，走进了英国著名的肯特大教堂和利兹城堡。这个季节，一路风景如画，不约花开，只赏秋叶，有红有白，有绿有黄。

　　当阵阵清风吹起片片金黄的树叶，刹那间空中的舞动，如华尔兹般优雅而美妙。从风起飞舞到风止落下，我看到了树叶飞舞时的潇洒和落地时的从容。看着眼前这一地的金黄，我想到了，这就是生命的过程，世间万物本循环，一切生命缘起性空。枝头的树叶缘于树根和树干的支撑，根茎的生长又缘于大地的滋养，而落叶归根正是起点和终点的循环，这叫"不生不灭，不垢不净，不增不减"，同时这也是生命的生生不息，道法自然。

　　树在四季的轮回中生长，人在善恶的道路上行驶，以怎样的姿态走完人生的旅程，这是我们人类必须要思考的一个问题。生命的

品质在于体证，也就是说在于实践，实践代表行为的落实，而行为的落实又决定我们所要去的地方。人只有明白道理，遵循真理，才有可能回归自然。如同树叶一般，当季节来临之际，风起的时候在空中潇洒自如，风止的时候在地上随遇而安，这就是自在随缘。

On the National Day and the Mid-Autumn Festival, the rare two holidays, I came to London, England. After an hour or so drive yesterday, I walked into the famous Kent Cathedral and Leeds Castle. All the way is of picturesque in this season, do not look at the blossom flowers, only admire autumn leaves, red and white, green and yellow.

When the breeze blows up the golden leaves, the flashing motion in the air is as elegant and wonderful as the Fahrenheit. From flying in the wind to falling in the wind, I saw the swagger of the leaves when they fly and the ease when they fall. Looking at the golden spot of this place, I thought of it. This is the process of life. In this world, everything is in circulation, and all lives are from empty. The leaves of the branches are supported by the roots and trunks. The growth of the roots and stems is nourished by the earth. The fallen leaves are to the ground root where is the starting point and the end point of the leaves forming a cycle. This is called "no growth, no death; no dirt, no stain; no increase, no decrease". At the same time, this is also the endless life and the law of nature.

The tree grows in the reincarnation of the four seasons. The people walk on the road of good and evil, and how they walk through the journey of life. This is a problem that we humans must think about. The quality of life lies in physical evidence. That is to say, in practice. The practice represents the implementation of the act. And the implementation of the behavior determines where we're going. People can only return to the nature if they understand the truth and follow the truth. Like the leaves, when the season comes, when the wind rises, they will flow freely in the air. When the wind stops, they will be on the ground. It is free and easy.

56

"般若波罗蜜多" 之含义
The meaning of "Prajna Paramita"

般若者，智慧也；波罗蜜者，到达彼岸也
Prajna wisdom; and polom, on the other side

　　近些年，我去过很多企业，看见不少企业老板办公室的墙上都挂着《心经》，有手写版的，也有印刷版的，还有各种不同材质制作而成的。看到此现象，我在想，也许有些人对《心经》是不解其意的，但他们仍然喜欢。这其中有用来装饰的，有想得到吉祥保佑的，也有真正理解并由衷喜爱的。种种不同的心念，都以挂在墙上的相同形式显现。

　　《心经》的全称是《般若波罗蜜多心经》，我知道大多数挂在墙上的人都不解这其中的含义。般若波罗蜜是梵语的译音，所以初读者很难理解。

　　般若，指的是一种极高的智慧境界。般若智慧是凡夫通过不间断、深入学习和实践，从而逐渐进入一个透彻宇宙人生真理的境界。

　　波罗蜜多，是指由凡夫到圣人的境界。这个智慧境界的人，虽身处世间，但心不住于世间。从凡夫的此岸到达圣人的彼岸，是真正消除一切苦厄，无忧无虑，无生无死，欢乐自在的解脱境界。所以，《般若波罗蜜多心经》的含义就是：般若者，智慧也；波罗蜜者，到达彼岸也。

In recent years, I went to a lot of companies and saw many of the corporate bosses' offices hanging the *Heart Sutra*, written in hand, printed, and made of various materials. From this phenomenon, I was thinking that some people may not understand the *Heart Sutra*, but they still like it. Among these are those that are used for decoration, those that want to be fortune, and those that are truly understood and loved. All kinds of different thoughts are expressed in the same form on the wall.

The full name of the *Heart Sutra* is the *Prajna Paramita Sutra*. I know that most people hanging it on the wall do not understand the meaning of this topic. Prajna Paramita is a Sanskrit transliteration, so it is difficult for beginners to understand.

Prajna refers to a very high level of wisdom. Prajna wisdom is a mortal world that has gradually gone through a deep and thorough study and practice so as to gradually enter the truth of a thoroughgoing life in the universe.

Palomido refers to the realm from the mortal to the saint. Those who are in this world of wisdom, although they are in the world, their minds cannot live in the world. From the shore of the mortal reaches the other side of the saints, it is the realm of liberation that truly eliminates all the bitterness, no fear, no concern, no living, no death, joy at ease. Therefore, the meaning of the *Prajna Paramita Sutra* is: prajna wisdom; and polom, on the other side.

57

无为而无所不为
Inaction (non-doing) but all have actions

正因为虚空无穷之大，而妙有才能无穷之多

It is precisely because that the void is infinite,
and only wonderful things can be infinitely numerial

　　说到无为而无所不为，每个人都在用自我的意识和思维去认识和想象，殊不知这样的自我意识是建立在自身现有的认知程度上的。现有的认知是没有如实表现宇宙人生，以及整个世间的真正实相的，因为我们没有真正用心去读经典，没有真正用心去实践认识，去再实践再认识。我们完全没有体悟到宇宙人生真正的实相，就去把握和应用，所以现有的意识、思维、推理、认知、想象都是虚幻的，都是如露亦如电的梦幻泡影。

　　真正意义上的无为而无所不为，是"照见五蕴皆空"之后的无为而大有所为，这种境界，不单是思想，而是通过思想指导行为的切实有效的结果所在。

要做到无为，首先要忘掉自我，只有忘掉自我，才能"照见五蕴皆空"。五蕴指色、受、想、行、识，这是构成我们身体的五个元素。空，并非有人理解的财、名、利等都空，对财、名、利，我们不可执着，也决不能玩空（完空），这样的空会使我们的生命也随之而断灭。没有了生命，也没有了修行的载体，更谈不上无所不为。

真正的无为是忘掉自我，为他人的幸福而充满活力、朝气蓬勃、生龙活虎地去践行，让生命之花在品质中绽放。

正如我们的肉身，它也只能在虚空中存在，在虚空中由生到死，完成转化的过程。身体死了又转化成其他的物种。相对虚空来说，物质永远是"不生不灭，不垢不净，不增不减"的。正因为虚空无为，所以虚空无所不为地包罗万象。浩瀚宇宙谁为大，虚空为大。正因为虚空无穷之大，而妙有才能无穷之多。

When it comes to "inaction but all have actions", everyone is using his own consciousness and thinking to understand and imagine, but they do not know that such self-consciousness is based on their current level of awareness. The current understanding is that there is no true representation of the universe and the real reality of the entire world, because we did not really try to read the classics, we did not really try our best to practice the knowledge, and then practice and recognise again. We do not realize the real reality of the universe, and we grasp and apply it. Therefore, the existing consciousness, thinking, reasoning, cognition, and imagination are all imaginary, and they are all like dew also like electricity, dreamlike bubbles.

The real sense of "inaction and all have actions", is the inaction but can achieve the great success according to the law "see that the five aggregates are empty" afterwards. This realm is not only an idea but an effective result of ideological guidance.

To achieve inaction, we must first forget ourselves. Only by forgetting ourselves can we "illuminate the five aggregates empty". The five aggregates mean color, acceptance, thought, behavior, and cognition that are the five elements that make up our body. This "empty" is not the empty of the money, names, profits, etc that the people understand. We must not be obstinate in terms of finances, names, and interests, and we must never chase for the empty (complete empty). Such an empty space will lead our lives to death. If there is no life, there will be no carrier for our spiritual practice, not to mention everything.

The true inaction is to forget about oneself, to be full of vitality for others' happiness, to be full of vigor and vitality, to live alive, and to let the flowers of life bloom in quality.

Just like our body, it can only exist in the void, from birth to death in the void, to complete the process of transformation. The body died and reincarnate. In contrast to the void, the material is always "not bear immortal, not dirty, not clean, not increase, not decrease". Because the void is inaction, the void is embracing all. In the vast universe, what is the biggest? The void is the biggest! It is precisely because that the void is infinite, and only wonderful things can be infinitely numerial.

58

如何面对疾病与死亡
How to deal with illness and death

明了真理的人，健康长寿不难，无疾而终也不难
It is not difficult for the people who understand the truth of
the universe to live a long and healthy life

　　人人免不了生病，人人免不了死亡。疾病没人想有，死亡令人恐惧。人生在世，到底怎样一个活法才能少生病？对于死亡，人人都知道它迟早会来，人们都很无奈地在恐惧中等待着它的到来，但人世间的确有方法让人健康长寿，也的确有方法让人不畏死亡。这样的方法在经典里，在医书《黄帝内经》里都能找到答案。遗憾的是，现代人大多不读经典，也读不懂经典，讲《黄帝内经》的人很多，但真正做到的人很少。因此面对疾病和死亡，从医者也无法战胜，这难道不是人类的悲哀吗？

　　说到经典，人们很自然地会联想到宗教，包括佛教、道教、伊斯兰教、天主教等，每一个教派都有其教礼、教仪和经典。在此，

我想说明的是，疾病与健康、生与死，其实跟任何宗教无关，千百年来，人们并没有因有了宗教而避免疾病和死亡。各大宗教之所以能不断地传承，是因为有识之士认清了宗教里所传承的核心就是经典，而经典是人类智慧的结晶，是宇宙、天地、人生的真理。各教派仅仅是以各种不同的形式，把经典传承了下来。因此人类地球上的各个国家，都给予了宗教信仰的自由。

例如《道德经》，能真正读懂并遵照执行者，一定能健康长寿，也一定能解决对死亡恐惧的问题。因此对于明了真理的人，健康长寿不难，无疾而终也不难。疾病与健康，出生与死亡，是人生之大事，但由于我们不明真相，往往都忽略了大事而抓住了小事。

Everyone is inevitably sick, and everyone cannot avoid death. No one wants disease, death is terrifying. Life is alive. How can a living method in the end be less sick and healthy? With regard to the disease and death, everyone knows that it will come sooner or later. People are reluctantly awaiting its arrival in fear. However, there are ways to make people live healthy and longevity. There are indeed ways that the people do not fear death. This method can be found in the classic, in the medical book *Huang Di Nei Jing*. Unfortunately, most people in modern times do not read classics and can't read classics. There are many people who talk about the *Huang Di Nei Jing*, but there are very few people who really do. Therefore, in the face of disease and death, is it not the sorrow of mankind that doctors can not overcome?

When it comes to the classics, the people naturally associate with religions, including Buddhism, Taoism, Islam, Catholicism, etc. Each sect has its own rituals, teaching instruments,

and classics. Here, I would like to explain the disease and health, life and death. In fact, that have nothing to do with any religion. For thousands of years, people have not avoided disease and death because of religion. The reason why the major religions can be passed down is because the people of insight recognize that the core of religion is the classics. Classics are the crystallization of human wisdom and the truth of the universe, the world, and the life. Each sect only inherited the classics in various forms. Therefore, all countries on the human earth have given freedom of religious belief.

For example, if the people who can truly understand and execute The *Tao Te Ching*, they will surely live a long and healthy life. It will certainly solve the terror problem of death. Therefore, it is not difficult for the people who understand the truth of the universe to live a long and healthy life. Disease and health, birth and death are major events in life. However, because we do not understand the truth, we often neglect important matters and catch small things.

59

因缘无处不在的真相
The truth that Karma is everywhere

欲知前世因，今生受者是，欲知来世果，今生做者是

To know the causes of past lives, the recipient of this life is,
to know the consequences of the future, the performer of this life is

常言道：万事万物因缘合。几乎人人都知道种善因结善缘，种恶因结恶缘，今天所面临的一切是因缘所致。比如今天谈生意，遇到一个骗子，而自己当时就相信了骗子，结果血本无归。这时后悔莫及，怨恨恼怒油然而生，这是人们普遍的反应，而明理者这时会安静地从自身找到问题的根本。

事出有因，因在哪里？因在过往的起心动念和行为里。正所谓"欲知前世因，今生受者是，欲知来世果，今生做者是"，这里所说的前世，不仅是指我们生命的前世，它也指我们今生过往的所思、所想、所做、所为；今生也指今天、当下、此刻；来世也指明天、后天、下月、明年、后年。这句话是要我们明白，善缘、恶缘都是我们自己造就的。

再说骗子的因缘，来者之所以骗你，是你和他之前由于某一事种下了不善之因，今天他来讨债。但是，他今天以欺骗的手段来行事，从而又种下了不善之因，这个因迟早会让他骗来的财也留不住，即使留住了，发达了，这表面看上去是好事，却隐藏着更大的后患。这种不善之因，迟早会有不善之缘不请自来，祸端的发生往往就是如此。这就是因缘无处不在的真相。

As the saying goes: everything depends on causes. Almost everyone knows that the goodness is due to good karma and the evil is caused by bad karma. All that is faced today is due to causes. For example, when you talk about business today, you meet a liar and you believe in a liar. At this time, it was regretful that resentment and anger had arisen spontaneously. This was a popular response, and the reasoner would now quietly find the root of the problem.

What happened with a cause, but where is the cause? The cause is in the past, when you started to think and act. The so-called "To know the causes of past lives, the recipient of this life is, to know the consequences of the future, the performer of this life is." The past lives referred to here do not necessarily refer to the past lives of our lives. It also refers to what we have thought, considered, done, and commited in this life; this life also refers to today, the present, and the moment; the afterlife also indicates the day, the day after tomorrow, the next month, the next year, and the year after. This sentence is for us to understand that good karma and evil karma are created by ourselves.

Then come to the reason of the liar, the reason why the comer lied to you was because you and him had planted a cause for something bad because of a certain thing. Today, he came to collect debts. However, he acted today by means of deceit, which in turn planted a cause of misfortune. This would not allow him to retain his deceived money sooner or later. Even if he retained it, he was developed. It seems to be a good thing on the surface. But it hides bigger problems inside. This kind of bad karma will sooner or later come without invitation. This is often the case with disaster. This is the truth of karma everywhere.

60

少欲知足，进入更高境界
Content with less desire, enter the higher realm

顺则成钢，逆则成仙
Going along people's habits is the "mortal",
acting in the "converse" is the saint

"顺则成人，逆则成仙。"这句话的意思是告诫人们修身之道在于修心。凡夫俗子究其一生也不明白生命的真谛，这就导致我们在整个生命过程中，很容易地顺着我们的身心之欲去思考和行动。

例如，我们有财色之欲、名食之欲、睡懒之欲，这些在我们看来都是正常的人生行为，却恰恰是我们永远无法摆脱人道的基本法则。人生就是财、色、名、食、睡，脱离了这些基本法则，生命似乎就没有了意义。同时，这也是人的精神和物质境界，人在这个层面上循环往复，不断地重复着财、色、名、食、睡。我们根本就不知道，有一种与之相反的方法，可以让我们脱离人道，进入"仙道"。

所谓"仙道"指的是比人更高层次的精神和物质境界。进入这个境界需要人做到少欲知足。就财、色、名、食、睡而言，我们不可以去除，也不可能去除，怎么办呢？

在财上，取之有道，用之也要有道。对自己适可而止，其余的奉献出去，利益他人。在色上，要节制欲望，洁身自爱。在名上，不求利己，一心利益他人，名气不求自来。在食上，民以食为天，食不可不求，但决不妄求，多食不益，确保健康长寿。在睡上，睡眠不可缺，科学说要保证八小时，其实不用，有四个小时的深度睡眠足矣，久卧伤气，现实中睡眠时间过长是身体不健康的表现，而修行极高的人可以以坐代睡。所以，从人到"仙"就是这样的过程。

Going along people's habits is the "mortal", acting in the "converse" is the saint. This sentence is to admonish people to cultivate themselves by practicing their own minds. Everyone in the mortal world does not understand the true meaning of life. This leads us to easily think and act along our physical and mental desires throughout our lives.

For example, we have the desires for whealth, lust, fame, food, sleep, and laziness. These are normal behaviors in our eyes, but it is precisely the basic principle that we can never get rid of humanity. Life is of money, lust, fame, food, and sleep. From these basic rules, life seems to have no meaning. At the same time, this is also the spiritual and material realm of human beings. People circulate at this level and continue to repeat their wealth, lust, fame, food, and sleep. We do not know at all that there is a way opposite to it, which will allow us to break away from humanity and enter on the path of "fairy".

The so-called "path of immortal" refers to a higher level of spiritual and material realm than humans. To enter this realm requires people to do with less desire, to be content. As to whealth, lust, fame, food, or sleep. It is impossible to remove, nor can we remove them. What should we do?

In finance, there must be a right way to take and a correct way to use. To oneself it is enough to afford, and the rest to be devoted to others. In sexy, you should control your lust and keep your body clean. In the fame, we don't seek self-serving, we are interested in others, and our reputation is not sought. In food, it is the paramount necessity of the people. One can't stop asking for food, but you can not make presumptuous demand. It's bad to eat more, to ensure a long and healthy life. In sleep, sleep can not be lacking, the science says to guarantee eight hours, in fact, there is no need, four hours of deep sleep is enough, long lying injury, in reality, long-sleeping people are unhealthy performance, and the people with very high spiritual practices can sit for sleep. Therefore, it is such a process from human to the "immortal".

6I

中国手工制作的魅力
Chinese handmade charm

穿梭了无数的来回，每一次的来回都凝聚着匠人们的心血

Shuttle back and forth numerous loops,
each time round and round embodies the hearts of the craftsmen

　　在美国访问期间，我人生第一次进入一个崭新的世界，零距离见到美国总统特朗普先生，进入最高级的社交场合。原本以为那个聚集美国政商要人于一起的场合是绚丽多姿、争芳斗艳的，但当我身着一件手工制作的中国式绣花连衣裙进入晚宴时，许多美国人都不约而同地赞叹我的裙子漂亮。这时，我才下意识地关注了一下其他人的穿着打扮，我发现现场的人们真没什么特别的，无论男士还是女士，并非电影电视里看到的那么凸显，反而我身着的中国式绣花连衣裙格外的引人注目。

　　是的，无论怎样的剪裁方法制作出来的服装，都赶不上千针万线走出来的手工制作。尤其是花朵的魅力，那是绣花人的匠心所至，多达五十种颜色的丝线，穿梭了无数个来回，每一次的来回都凝聚着匠人们的心血，每个花朵都包含着匠人们美好的愿景和辛勤的汗水。此刻，花朵的装饰和裙摆的飘逸，无不散发着中国气息。

　　当我手执酒杯，轻盈行走在宴会之中，在众人的称赞之下，我开始无比的自信。

During my visit to the United States, I entered a brand-new world for the first time. I met Trump, the highest social status, for the first time, and entered the highest social scene for the first time. Originally I thought that the occasion where American political and business leaders gathered together was supposed to be brilliant and colorful, but when I was wearing a handmade Chinese-style embroidered dress to enter the dinner party, many Americans praised me at the same time. The skirt is beautiful. At this time, I was subconsciously paying attention to the dress of other people. I found that the people at the scene were really nothing special. No matter whether men or women are not outstanding seen in the film and television. On the contrary I was eye- catching wearing a Chinese-style embroidery dress.

Yes, no matter what kind of the garments made out with tailoring methods, it's not worth the dress of tens of thousands of lines out of hand-made. Especially the charm of flowers, it is the embroider's ingenuity, up to fifty colors of silk thread, shuttle back and forth numerous loops, each time round and round embodies the hearts of the craftsmen, each flower contains craftsmen a good vision and hard work. At this moment, the decoration of the flowers and the flowing skirts all exude Chinese flavor.

When I held the glass of wine in my hand and walked lightly in the banquet, under the praise of everyone, I began to feel very confident.

工匠精神
——秋山利辉的成功之道
Craftsmanship: Akiyama Akihiro's success

工匠精神，利而无往，往而不害，安平泰
Craftsman spirit is beneficial everywhere for everything,
without a harm, hence comes peace

在日本，一个叫秋山利辉的人，他创建了一家木工专业定制的企业。这个小到只有 34 人的企业，却创下了年销售额 11 亿日元的价值，这令人惊叹的业绩，来源于秋山利辉不同凡响的企业管理模式。

这是一个学习型企业，这里规定男女一律剃寸头、禁止玩手机、禁止谈恋爱、禁止接受父母钱物、每天背法则三四遍、每天必须写总结反省，以及八年零假期，学满八年，第九年开始独立打天下。面对如此严格的管理，我想很多人是不可能接受的，但作为一家企业的管理者，我深知秋山利辉的良苦用心。

男女剃寸头，这是让学徒断除男女色相的分别之心，进而不起色欲。禁止玩手机，是让学徒不受世间杂尘的污染，保持清净之心，从而专注学习。禁止谈恋爱，是让学徒在学习期间不因恋爱而浪费宝贵的时间。不接受父母钱物，是让学徒养成自食其力的信念，从而学到真实的本领，才能使父母心安理得。每天背法则三四遍，不间断地重复背诵，守住戒律，增强能量。每天写总结反省，"君子终日乾乾，夕惕若厉，无咎"。八年零假期，每天工作没有间断，从而养成坚韧不拔、终生勤劳的优良作风，使学徒终生受益。这真是智者的管理模式。

　　这种形同出家人的管理模式中诞生了最为真实的实际效益——年销售额 11 亿日元。这些效益来源于日本皇室、日本宫内厅、迎宾馆、国会议事堂和知名大饭店。这就是秋山利辉的成功之道。工匠精神，利而无往，往而不害，安平泰。

In Japan, a person named Akiyama Akihiro, he founded a company that is specialized in carpentry. This small company of only 34 employees has set a value of 1.1 billion yen (Yen) in annual sales. This impressive performance has come from Akiyama's extraordinary business management model.

This is a learning enterprise, where men and women are required to shave their heads with short spiky hair, stop playing with cell phones, and stop falling in love, refrain from accepting the money and materials from parents, recite the law three or four times a day, write a summary and introspection every day, and have zero vacation for eight years, after study for eight years, and become independent in the ninth year. Faced with such strict management, I think many people are not able to accept it. But as a manager of a company, I know very well what Akiyama Akihiro is doing.

Men and women shave their heads with short spiky hair, this is a separate mind that allows apprentices to cut off men and women's hue, and can't afford lust. It is forbidden to play with mobile phones. It is for apprentices to be free from the pollution of the world's dust and to maintain a clean mind, so that they can concentrate on learning. It is forbidden to fall in love so that apprentices do not waste precious time during their studies. Do not accept parental money and materials, and allow apprentices to develop self-supporting beliefs so that they can learn real skills and make their parents feel at ease. Every day, recite the regulations three or four times, continuous repetition of recitation, guarding the commandments, enhance energy. Every day they write a summary of their reflection. The gentleman will continue to work day after day. In the 8 years and zero holidays, there are no interruptions in work every day, so as to develop a good style of perseverance and diligence, which will benefit apprentices for the rest of their lives. This is really a wise man's management model.

This kind of monk management model has produced the most real practical benefits-annual sales of 1.1 billion yen (Yen). These benefits come from the Japanese royal family, the Japanese Imperial Palace Hall, the guest house, the National Assembly Hall, and famous hotels. This is Akiyama's success. Craftsman spirit is beneficial everywhere for everything, everything can be achieved smoothly and beneficially without a harm, hence comes peace.

63

实体经济与虚拟经济缺一不可

The real economy and virtual economy
are indispensable

虚拟经济为阴，实体经济为阳。一阴一阳谓之道

The virtual economy is Yin (negative) and the real economy
is Yang (positive). One Yin and one Yang mean the Tao

最近听做实体经济的人说，发展实体经济是国家的未来；做虚拟经济的人则说，虚拟经济是强国的最好方法。其实这两者的言论都过于偏激，都是就局部而论局部的言论。

如果我们站在国家的层面来看待实体经济和虚拟经济的问题，就会清楚地认识到：实体经济和虚拟经济是事物阴阳的两个方面。在此，虚拟经济为阴，实体经济为阳。一阴一阳谓之道，阴阳是构成事物的两个方面。人世间所有的事物，都是在阴阳之间的相互促进和相互制约中向前发展变化的。这道理很简单，孤阳不生，孤阴不长，男女阴阳相合才能生育后代，生生不息。实体经济和虚拟经济同样如此。对于国家而言，实体经济和虚拟经济是不可缺少的两个部分，阴阳相合、虚实相应，才能真正促进国民经济的良性发展。从事物的局部决定事物整体的发展方向是不对的，学会从整体看局部才能有效地把握未来的发展方向，在世界经济激烈的竞争中立于不败之地。

从某种意义上说，实体经济离不开虚拟经济的助力，虚拟经济也离不开实体经济的支撑，两者缺一不可。

Recently those who do the real economy say that the development of the real economy is the future of the country; those who do the fictitious economy say that the virtual economy is the best way to strengthen the country. In fact, both of these remarks are too extreme. They are all partial comments on the topic.

If we look at the real economy and virtual economy at the national level, we will clearly recognize that the real economy and the virtual economy are two aspects of the Yin and Yang of things. Here, the virtual economy is Yin (negative) and the real economy is Yang (positive). One Yin and one Yang mean the Tao. Say that Yin and Yang are two aspects of things. All things in the world are moving forward in the mutual promotion and mutual restraint between Yin and Yang. This principle is very simple, The solitary Yang is not producing, the solitary Yin is not growing, and the Yin and Yang combination, the men and women combination can produce offspring to survive. The real economy and the virtual economy are the same. For the country, the real economy and the virtual economy are two indispensable components. Congruence between Yin and Yang and the corresponding real and virtual can really promote the sound development of the national economy. It is wrong to determine the overall development direction of things from the locality of things. Learning to look at the local from the whole can effectively grasp the direction of future development, so as to be undefeated in the fierce competition of the world economy.

In a sense, the real economy is inseparable from the support of the virtual economy, and the virtual economy is inseparable from the support of the real economy. Both are indispensable.

64

敬天爱人
Worship the heaven, love the people

平等之心，善待一切大众
The mind of equality is
to kindly treat all people well

随着中国传统文化的悄然复苏，"敬天爱人"这个词语常常可以看到。顾名思义，敬天就是对天要有敬畏之心，爱人就是对人要有善良慈悲之举。

在此，我们首先要明白天的含义。天是什么？天怎样描述？有人能一语讲清楚吗？圣人老子告诉我们，天是道的产物，道不但生育天地，同时也推动了日月的运行，滋养了万物的生长。道的能量无穷之大，但我们只能看见道所产生的天地万物，却无法看见道的形象。天同样如此，当我们仰望天空，只能看到不断变化的各种云彩，而天的形状却不得而知。但有一点我们可以知道，天地阴阳造化，生育了万事万物，山川河流，草木丛林。天大，地大，人是天地所生，人也大。天地是人类的父母，敬天是我们的本分。

既然人类是天地的孩子，那相亲相爱就是我们对天地的一份孝心。用善良慈悲对待每一个人很难做到，因为分别心，让我们对那些有恩于我们的人和那些可怜的人容易产生慈悲之心，但对那些伤害我们的人就很难慈悲以待。"平等大悲"是难以做到的。

平等之心，善待一切大众，那是圣人的境界，那是大智慧的行为。敬天是本分，爱人是德行，此两者是人类获取福报的通行证。

With the quiet recovery of traditional Chinese culture, we often see the term: "Worship the heaven, Love the people". As the name implies, "worship the heaven" means having respect for the heaven, and "love the people" means having kindness and compassion for others.

Here, we must first understand the meaning of the heaven. What is the heaven? How to describe the heaven? Can someone speak clearly? The sage Laozi tells us that the heaven is the product of Tao. Not only it gives the birth of the heaven and the earth, but it also promotes the operation of the sun and the moon, nourishing the growth of all things. The energy of the Tao is infinite, but we can only see the things that the Tao generated, but we cannot see the image of the Tao. The same is true for heaven. When we look up at the sky, we can only see the ever-changing clouds, but the shape of the heaven is unknown. However, one thing we can know is that the heaven and the earth are created by Yin and Yang, and there are tens of thousands of things, mountains and rivers, and grass, jungles and trees. The heaven and the earth are large and great, the people are born in the heaven and the earth, and the people are also great. The heaven and the earth are the parents of mankind. Respecting the heavens is our duty.

Since humans are the children of the heaven and the earth, love for others is our filial piety to the heaven and the earth. Treating everyone with kindness and compassion is very difficult to do, because we have separation minds that we can be compassionate for those who are interested in us and those who are poor, but it is difficult for us to be merciful for those who harm us. It is difficult to achieve "Equality and great sadness".

The mind of equality is to kindly treat all people well. It is the realm of saints. It is the act of great wisdom. It is the duty of respecting the heavens, and the love is the virtue. These two are the pass for humans to obtain blessings.

65

恒变的世界，不变的道
The constant change of the world,
the changeless Tao

变化是常态
Change is the norm,
and no change is false

现实生活中，我们常常有感于人生无常、世事无常，说到底，人世间就没有一件不变的事，也没有一个不变的人。变化是常态，不变是虚妄。

在这个变化无常的世界里，我们学会怎样把握好自己的人生，学会怎样以不变应万变来使自己摆脱烦恼、忧伤和悲观之苦，这是一个由认识到实践的过程。"一阴一阳谓之道"，何为阴？何为阳？何为道？

阴阳是事物变化和发展的两个方面，天地阴阳造化万物，万物生灭永不停止；男女阴阳相合，繁衍后代，生生不息代代相传，这其中的奥妙乃道法自然。"寂兮寥兮，独立而不改，周行而不殆"，道生万物，而不恃其有万物；道之功德无可计量，却从不自以为大，所以道才能具备这种强大的力量。

阴阳变化无始无终，大千世界变化无穷。恒变的世界，不变的道。

In real life, we often feel a sense of impermanence in life and impermanence in the world. In the final analysis, there is no constant thing in the world and there is no one who does not change. Change is the norm, and no change is false.

In this volatile world, we learn how to grasp our own lives and learn how to free ourselves from suffering, grief and pessimism without change. This is a process from recognition to practice. "One Yin and one Yang is the Tao." What is Yin? What is Yang? What is the Tao?

Yin and Yang are two aspects of the change and development of things. The heaven and the earth, Yin and Yang make things, and the birth and destruction of all things never stop. Yin and Yang of men and women reproduce their offspring, and they continue to live from generation to generation. The mystery is the Tao of nature. "Lonely, independent but not changed, walking without blasphemy". The Tao produces everything, and does not care for everything. The merits of the Tao are incalculable but never self-righteous, That's why the Tao is so powerful.

Yin and Yang changes have no beginning or end, and the vast world is changing. The constant change of the world, changeless is Tao.

秋言物语

66

获得幸福的方法
How to get happiness

真理就是宇宙人生真实存在的本来面目

The truth is the true law of the real existence of the universe and life

说到底，人世间所有的人都在追求幸福，每一个人都在为幸福而奔波劳累，但现实的生活和工作常常带给我们失落、烦恼和忧伤，真正能够如愿以偿的事情很少发生，因此我们常常感叹人生十有八九不如人意。这是为什么呢？

在我看来，这是因为人们偏离了真理的航线，而走入了迷途。真理就是宇宙人生真实存在的本来面目，它不以人的意志为转移，也不因人的信与不信而改变。真理不存在信与不信，只取决于人们对其的认识和了解程度，而人们的认识和了解程度又决定了自己的幸福指数。

因此，人生要想获得真正的幸福，其根本是要找到获得幸福的方法。首先我们需要了解自己有没有获得幸福的能力，这其中除了生活和工作能力之外，还包括是否具备乐善好施、慈悲助人、善于付出、不善索取、奉献多于收获等优良品质，这些都是我们获得幸福的方法。我这样讲，估计有人不信，信与不信都取决于福报，福报大的人信受笃行，福报小的人半信半疑，没有福报的人完全不信，这就叫道法自然。

After all, all the people in the world are pursuing happiness. Everyone is working hard for happiness. However, the real life and work often bring us loss, trouble, and sorrow. The things that really get what we want are rare. Therefore, we often sigh that life is not so good nine times out of ten. Why is that?

In my opinion, this is because that the people have deviated from the route of the truth and they have been lost. The truth is the true law of the real existence of the universe. It is not shifted by the will of man, nor changed by the faith and unbelief of man. The truth does not exist trust and unbelief, it depends only on people's understanding and awareness of their level, and the degree of the people's understanding and awareness determines their own happiness index.

Therefore, if the life is to achieve true happiness, it is fundamental to find a way to obtain happiness. First of all, we need to understand whether we have the ability to obtain the happiness, including whether we have the good qualities of the benevolent charity, compassion, goodness in giving, and giving more than harvest, in addition to our ability to live and work. All of these are the methods to obtain the happiness. I say this, it is estimated that some people do not believe. Whether they believe or not depends on the blessings they have. People with plentiful blessings believe my words and practise earnestly, people with few blessings are rather dubious of my words, and people without any blessing don't believe my words at all. This is called "Tao follows the nature".

67

电影更迭，时代变迁

Movies change, times change

那个时代的电影在我心田种下了正义、无私和大无畏的英雄种子

The movie of that era planted the seeds of heroes of justice, selflessness, and fearlessness in my mind

秋言物语

昨晚看了电影《无问西东》，这是继《芳华》后又一部能够深入人心、可以触动灵魂的国产影片。

电影是我打小就十分喜爱的文艺作品。记得小时候，电影院很少，影片远不及现在多，我常常搬着小凳子，背着小我五岁的妹妹，欢天喜地地坐在露天坝看电影。记忆尤其深刻的是《英雄儿女》《永不消逝的电波》《闪闪的红星》，那个时代的电影在我心田种下了正义、无私和大无畏的英雄种子。现在想想，那个时代的电影有着太多的回味……

随着改革开放的不断深入，电影业在西方文化和经济浪潮的冲击下，有些变得物欲横流、肆无忌惮，色情、暴力、恐怖影片相继出现。这一时期的特殊现象，的确让人迷惑，甚至堕落。一时间，如此喜爱电影的我渐渐地消失在迷茫的风雨中，电影在我的生活中变得淡然无味，豪华的影院不及我童年的土坝，强大的明星阵容也引不起我看他们的兴趣，再高超的拍摄技术也只瞬间惊异便成过眼云烟。心物各东西，灵魂飘浮两茫然……

近来一部《战狼Ⅱ》再次引起了我的兴趣，它把我从露天坝子推进了豪华舒适的影院。一部《芳华》，又一部《无问西东》让我找回了儿时从电影获得的感觉：正义、善良、勇敢和无私。

Last night I saw a movie "Forever Young". This is another domestic film that can touch the soul after "Fang Hua".

The film is a literary and artistic work that I loved very much since I was a child. I remember when I was a child, there were very few cinemas, and the films were far less than they are now. I often took a small stool and carried my sister five-years younger than me, and I happily sat in the open dam to watch movies with joy. The most profound memory is the "Heroic Children", "Everlasting Waves", "The Glowing Red Star". The movie of that era planted the seeds of heroes of justice, selflessness, and fearlessness in my mind. Now that I think about it, the movies of that era have me too much aftertaste...

With the continuous deepening of reform and opening up, the film industry has become materialistic and unscrupulous under the impact of Western culture and economic waves, and pornography, violence, and horror films have appeared one after another. The special phenomenon of this period is indeed confusing and even depraved. For a time, I was so fond of movies that I gradually disappeared in the turbulent winds and rain. The movie became indifferent to my life, the vegetation was no longer alive, the fish and water were separated, the luxurious cinema was less than my childhood earth dam. The strong star lineup also does not attract me to see their interest, and the superb shooting technique is only a momentary surprise, and it becomes a cloud of smoke. All things in the mind and soul, floating in separately and unexpectedly...

Recently, a "Wolf of War II" opened the door to my interest, and it pushed me from the open-air dam to a luxurious and comfortable cinema. A "Fang Hua" and yet another "Forever Young" reminded me to regain the feeling I had obtained from movies in my childhood: justice, kindness, courage, and selflessness.

68

人的因缘造就时代
Human karma creates the era

我们自己种的因，当然要由我们自己来承受

The cause of our own planting, of course,
must be borne by ourselves

我想大多数人都在一些媒体发布的文章中，看见一批"50后""60后"在抱怨自己生不逢时：赶上"上山下乡"，赶上"高考如千军万马过独木桥"，赶上"计划生育"，赶上"下岗潮"等等不如人意的事情。

　　从事物的表象来看，这的确是"50后""60后"不可否认的亲身经历，但人世间任何事情的发生都是因缘决定的。"50后""60后"为什么会赶上这个时代呢？凡事物因缘合，有前因才能有后果，前因是"50后""60后"这批人由于相同的善恶之因，而产生了相同的善恶之果。说到底就是"50后""60后"这批人在过去一生中都有着相同的善行和恶行，从而造就了一个属于"50后""60后"的时代。这一时代现象的发生，不是时代造就的，更不是时代强加给我们的，是我们自己的善恶之因决定了我们必定造就这样一个时代。我们自己种的因，当然要由我们自己来承受。

　　任何一个时代的现象都代表着这个时代的人们的过去和现在。同样，未来的时代怎样，也取决于我们这一时代的所思所行。任何一个时代都是人创造的，千百年来，人们谱写着历史的篇章，光辉灿烂与阴霾笼罩，都在同一时代互相碰撞、互相制约、互相促进，这就是道的阴阳之理。

秋言物语

I think in some articles published by the media, most people saw a group of people born in 1950s and 1960s complaining about their misfortunes: they were catching up with the "going up the mountain and going to the countryside", catching up with "College Entrance Examination like thousands of horses crossing a log bridge", catching up with the "family planning", catching up with the "lay-offs tide" and other things that are not satisfactory.

Judging from the appearance of things, this is indeed an undeniable personal experience in the post-50s and the 60s. However, the occurrence of anything in the world is determined by the cause. Why did you catch up with this era after 50 and 60? All things can be contingent due to their affinities. The premise is that the 50th and 60th generations of people have the same results of good and evil because of the same causes of good and evil. In the final analysis, the 50th and 60th generations of people in the past all had the same kind of good deeds and evil acts, thus creating an era that belongs to the 50s and 60s. The occurrence of this era is not caused by the times. What is more, it is not imposed on us by the times. Our own cause of good and evil determines that we must create such an era. The cause of our own planting, of course, must be borne by ourselves.

The phenomena of any era all represent the past and the present of people in this era. Similarly, what is the future era will also depend on the thinking and acting of our time. Every era is created by the people. For thousands of years, the people have written chapters in history. They are brilliant and hazy. They both collide with each other, constrain each other, and promote each other in the same era. This is the reason for the Yin and Yang of Tao.

69

历事炼心方见真假

Experience refines the mind to
see true or false

唯有觉悟的方法才能达到幸福的彼岸

Only by consciousness can reach
the other side of happiness

几天前，有人问我为什么最近看不见我的《秋言物语》了，我回答很快会有的。是啊，因为什么停顿了写作？因心受到了人和事的干扰。

此刻我静坐在去往新加坡的航班上，尽管机声轰鸣，但心安静了下来，渐渐地返观内照。"人心好静，而欲牵之。常能遣其欲，而心自静，澄其心而神自清……"对照《清净经》，我深深地感悟到历事炼心方见真假。近一个月的人事干扰完全来自于自身的执着，应有所住，而产生了有相分别妄想之心，因分别妄想而产生了烦恼，因烦恼而不得安宁，以至于几次提笔写《秋言物语》而又辍笔。这一个多月的心路历程充分地验证了自己的修行落在具体事物的表现并不合格，为此深深地忏悔！

行道之路千万条，唯有觉悟的方法才能到达幸福的彼岸。人人惧怕死亡，却很难有人明了生命为何无法摆脱死亡。千百年来，觉者知其机、明其理，从而以自利利他的方式快活地活着；愚人却因执着而自扰，忧愁烦恼，生老病死，随波逐流，生死相继……

A few days ago, someone asked me why he couldn't see my "Qiu's Monogatari" recently. I told him that I would soon have it. Yeah, because what stopped writing? Because my mind is disturbed by people and things.

At the moment I sat quietly on a flight to Singapore. Despite the sound of roaring, my mind was quiet, and I gradually returned to my inside view. "The minds of people are quiet, but their desires get involved. If the desires can be often controlled, their minds will be self quiet and cleansing..." In contrast to the *Clean Sutra*, I deeply feel that the experience of refining the mind to see true and false. In the past month or so, the personnel disturbance was entirely derived from my own perseverance that lived in the mind. Therefore they have created a sense of mutual delusion. The delusions cause troubles. The troubles cause being unsettled. Even a few times, I tried to write *Qiu's Monogatari* and put down the pen again. This more than a month of mental journey has fully verified the performance of my own practice on specific things, that is very unsatisfactory and I deeply regret this!

There are literally thousands of ways on the road. Only a method of consciousness can reach the other side of happiness. Everyone is afraid of death, but it is difficult for someone to understand why life cannot escape death. For thousands of years, the educated knew the reasoning, and thus lived happily in a self-benefiting manner; but the fools were perturbed by self-interest, sorrow and anguish, and birth, aged, sickness, death. With the tide, life and death follow one another.

70

一花一世界
One flower is one world

世界和平的愿景，就如同这满树花开，美妙入心田

The vision of world peace is just like the trees
in full bloom which are sweet and pleasant to our mind

　　纽约之行匆匆而过，回想前几天，当我们的车辆行走在街道上，透过车窗，眼前移动着开满白色小花的一棵棵不大不小的树，形状各异，花朵繁盛。尤为美妙的是：满树枝丫碎白花，未见绿叶展容颜。何树如此美妙？我们问开车的师傅，他回答说："不知道，我也觉得很奇怪，这树就是先开花后长叶。"噢，原来如此！花之先，叶之后，洁白典雅出尘垢。此刻，我脑海冒出一句多年未曾理解的话："一花一世界"，眼前这盛开在纽约街道两旁的白色小花是怎样的世界呢？

　　土地中生长，季节的来临、新鲜的空气、适当的温度、阳光的照耀、雨露的滋养、园丁的呵护、空间的生存和时间的限度，花朵的盛开，正是这一切的相互连接、共同协作，产生了眼前这如此美妙的景致。

　　"一花一世界"，宇宙万物本相连，完全没有孤立存在的任何事物。任何事物的出现都是聚合行为的结果，人与人、人与物、人与自

然，乃至国与国之间的任何状态，都是多元化的组合行为所产生的。因此，世界和平的愿景，就如同这满树花开，美妙入心田。这充满生机和如此美好的景况，需要各国人民共同协作，至善而至美……

My journey to New York has passed by, recalling that a few days ago, when our car driving along the streets, I saw through the windows the small trees passing by full of white flowers blooming in different shapes. What is particularly wonderful: the branches of those trees were full of branches and smashed white flowers, but without any green leaves showing face. What is such a wonderful tree? We asked the driver who drove the car. He replied, "No, I don't know. It's very strange for me, too. These trees are blooming first then coming into leaves." Oh, it is! The flowers first, the leaves after. The pure and elegant white originate from the dust. At this moment, one sentence that I could not comprehend over the years suddenly came to my mind: "One flower, one world". What kind of world is this white flower blooming on the streets of New York?

Growing in the soil, the coming of the season, the fresh air, the proper temperature, the sunshine, the nourishment of the rain and dew, the gardener's care, the survival in the space and the limits of time, the blooming of the flowers, it is precisely because that all these are interconnected and cooperated, such a wonderful view is created in front of us.

"One flower, one world", all things in the universe are connected with each other, and nothing exists in isolation at all. The emergence of anything is the result of aggregating behaviors. And any state between man and man, man and things, man and the nature, and even between state and state, is produced by the combination of pluralistic behaviors. Therefore, the vision of world peace is just like the trees in full bloom which are sweet and pleasant to our mind. This is full of vitality and such a beautiful scenario requires the cooperation of all peoples, in order to make it better and more wonderful...

71

人生的意义
——利他
The meaning of life: Altruism

有了这颗利他之心，人生才有了真正的意义

With this mind of altruism,
life has a real meaning

一觉醒来，凌晨五点，窗外淅淅沥沥的雨声伴随着阵阵蛙鸣，同时还有各种小鸟叽叽喳喳的欢笑声。啊！这难道不是天地宇宙间一首无比美妙而又如此和谐的大合唱吗？

我不禁下床走到窗边，撩开窗帘，隐约看见对面山顶上飘浮着乌云。当我的视线落在地面时，我看见乌云下、小雨中，环卫工人正推着小车在清理垃圾。我用手机拍了好几次，想抓住这一画面，但由于光线黑暗，我无法将环卫工人拍到镜头里。无奈之下，只想替辛勤的劳动者说一声：我的付出，您的舒适，请珍惜！

看着这眼前的情景，我又不禁想起前一阵在网上看到的一则消息，说某非常成功的大企业老板，在他的博客上发表了这样一条言论，他的人生是一个最大的失败，没有任何意义。

如此庞大的企业掌门人，顷刻间怎么产生了如此消极的情绪呢？他是在开悟人生？还是看破了红尘？或者是对人生有了新的认识？归根结底，当人进入某种物质层面的高度后，无论是人还是企业，都必须具备相应的文化内涵，有了文化才能有思想境界的提升，有了思想的高度才会产生一颗为他人谋幸福的心，有了这颗利他之心，人生才有了真正的意义，同时才能形成心灵快乐的源泉……早安！

When I woke up, at five in the morning, the sound of the rain outside the window accompanied with croaking of frogs, and birds chirping and laughing. Ah! Isn't it a wonderful and harmonious chorus of the universe?

I could not help getting out of bed, going to the window, lifting the curtains, and vaguely seeing clouds floating across the top of the mountain. When my eyes fell down on the ground, I saw that under the dark clouds and in the light rain, the sanitation workers were pushing cars to clean up the rubbish. I tried to take pictures several times with my mobile phone, but in vain due to the dim light. I couldn't get the sanitation workers into the camera. In desperation, I just want to say something for the hardworking workers: My contribution, your comfort, please cherish!

Looking at the scene in front of me, I could not help but think of a message I read on the Internet a time ago, saying that the boss of a very successful big company has made such a statement on his blog, he said his life was the biggest failure, and his life had no meaning.

How can such a huge company owner generate such pessimistic emotions? Is he enlightening the life? Or he becomes disillusioned with the mortal world? Or does he have real new knowledge on life? After all, when the people have achieved something in materials, both people and enterprises must have corresponding accomplishment in self-cultivation. With culture, they can have an ideological realm ascension. At the height of the thought, a mind of happiness for others is created. With this mind of altruism, life has a real meaning, and at the same time, it can produce the source of happiness of the mind... Good morning!

72

经历事情，觉悟人生
Experience is teacher of life

感恩缘起，感恩缘分

I'm grateful to the initiation of the fate,
to the fate

人生的每一段经历都是冥冥之中的定数，都是我们自己的前因后果，正如人生在世谁都免不了生病，这包括生理的疾病（物质）和心理的疾病（精神）。无论是生理的疾病还是心理的疾病都免不了"痛"，肉体之痛（物质）、心理之痛（精神），痛从何而来？

　　痛从知觉中来，痛因知觉而存在；知觉由心而来，知觉因心而存在，故"观是假的，痛是真的"。这里的观是观照，就是用智慧看清事物的本来面目。生病是真的，痛苦必然是真的。那为什么又说观是假的呢？正如我本修行人，但我并没有真正摆脱痛苦。我病了，我痛了，真的痛了！这时候观照就是假的，并没有进入菩萨深入谛观的层次。一句话：经历了痛苦，但并没有从痛苦中悟到真理，并没有真正看清事物的真相。"观"是思想，是思维修，简单来讲就是"想"。《心经》的第一个字就是观，观一切法，一切法包括我们的身心和身心以外的世界。

　　修行就是要实实在在地落实在日常生活的吃、喝、拉、撒、行、住、坐、卧、男女等具体行为中。观不能深入，不能观到事物的本质，故"观是假的，痛是真的"。当能够进入深入谛观的层次，方能悟得痛由觉知起，觉知由心起，无觉则无痛，无心觉知灭，心灭则法灭，法灭则烦恼忧悲伤苦灭，此时的观照是"五蕴皆空，渡一切苦厄"之境界……

　　感恩缘起，感恩缘分，感恩修行路上让我觉悟真理的每一个人！

Every experience in life is a definite number in the world. It is all our own cause and effect. Just as people in life will inevitably

suffer from diseases, including physical diseases (material) and psychological diseases (mental). Whether they are physical diseases, or psychological diseases are inevitable "pain", physical pain (material), psychological pain (mental). Where does the pain come from?

Pain comes from perception, and pain exists with perception; perception comes from the mind, and perception exists because of the mind. Therefore, "The view is fake, the pain is true", the view here is to observe, it is to see the true face of things with one's wisdom. Disease is real, and pain must be true. Then why do we say that the view is fake? Just as I am a practitioner, I have not really got rid of the pain. When I'm sick, I feel painful. It is really painful! At such time, the observation is false as it hasn't reached the level of Bodhisattva and deep insight. In a word: I experienced pain, but I did not realize the truth from pain, and did not really see the truth of things. The "observation" is a thought and cultivation of mind and simply saying "thinking". Therefore, the first word of *Heart Sutra* is observation which means observing all laws including our mind and body as well as the world beyond our mind and body.

Cultivation is to actually implement the specific behaviors of eating, drinking, defecating, urinating, walking, living, sitting, lying, men and women heterosexuality, etc. in daily life. The observation cannot be deep, and the essence of things cannot be observed. Therefore, "The view is false and the pain is true". When you can reach such level as deep insight, you can comprehend that the pain is from the perception and the perception is from the mind. If there's no perception, there's no pain; if there's no mind, there's no perception. If mind is gone, law is gone; if law is gone, then distress, worry and sorrow are all gone. At this time, the observation is the realm of "regarding all five skandhas as empty and crossing beyond all suffering and difficulty".

I'm grateful to the initiation of the fate, to the fate and to everyone that helped me comprehend the truth on the way of my cultivation!

73

感恩一切，成就未来
Grateful for everything to achieve the future

一切众生的因缘，我从心底感恩！

I am grateful to the karmas of
all people from the bottom of my mind

　　昨天，当我把《秋言物语》第七十二篇发在朋友圈后，就有人问我说："请教马总，为什么你在文章的结尾说'感恩缘起'，感恩缘分，感恩修行路上让我悟得真理的每一个人'？我的困惑是，你遇到的人当中一定不会都是善人吧？一定有伤害你的人和恶人吧？"就此问题，我在今天的《秋言物语》中回答：

　　首先，感恩之心是我们每一个人都应该具备的道德水准，也是心地善良的行为标志。问题的关键是感恩一切因缘，这其中包括好人、坏人、善人、恶人，一切众生的因缘，我都从心底感恩！

　　我的今天，鲜花、掌声、地位、荣誉，所有的成就都是众缘聚合而成的，这其中有善缘，也有恶缘；有众多的好人，也有个别的坏人；有君子，也有小人。就人的主观愿望，都想广结善缘，与好人交往，近君子远小人，但现实中，我们有时却事与愿违地遇到恶缘、坏人和小人，怎么办呢？

恶缘、坏人和小人，都是我们前世今生种善因或种恶因的果报，所以我们常言"来世报和现世报"。但怎样的情况是来世报，怎样的情况是现世报呢？告诉你，天网恢恢，疏而不漏，不是不报，时机未到，时机到了自然会报，这才是真理之道。

真理之道，不是你信与不信的问题，这是人们对它的认知和认可的问题。认可的人，自然会从因上下功夫，种善因，绝对会得善果。不认可的人，随性而行，在不知不觉中种下恶的种子，自然会天地报应，果报现前。这叫道法自然。

问题的关键是为什么要感恩恶缘、坏人和小人？恶缘是我们前世今生自己造就的，来了我们欣然接受，以善良的方式对待，这个

恶因就此了断，将来就成了善缘，这叫转恶为善。

坏人之所以被你遇到，有两种情况，一种是你的前因后果，另一种是你的愿力感召。有人发愿要成就一番事业，愿力越大，磨难越大，想要做好，必经魔考。坏人的出现，是增长你的善心、智慧、德行和能力的机会。小人心存不善，现实中通常会找你的软肋和漏洞，于是小人成了监督你的一双眼睛，所以在小人的帮助下你会不断向善。

因此，所有的成功都是众缘的聚合，这时方可领略在成功面前善恶同等、好坏无别，君子小人有别之行动、无别之成就。

所有因缘一并感恩！无比真挚的感恩！纯真纯善的感恩！

不夹杂任何私心杂念的感恩！以成功者的胸怀感恩一切！

Yesterday, when I issued the 72nd article of *Qiu's Monogatari* on the WeChat to the circle of my friends, someone asked me, "Ms. Ma, why did you say at the end of your article 'That I'm grateful to the initiation of the fate, to the fate and to everyone that helped me comprehend the truth on the way of my cultivation?' My confusion is that some people you encounter must not be all good ones? Must there be people who hurt you and the wicked?" On this question, I will response today in *Qiu's Monogatari* :

First of all, gratitude is a moral standard that everyone of us should have. It is also a sign of good behavior. The key to the issue is to feel grateful to all karmas, including good people, bad guys, kind-minded people and evil people. I am grateful to the karmas of all people from the bottom of my mind.

All my achievements nowadays, including flowers, applause, status and honor, are the result of the convergence of the karmas. Such karmas include both good ones and bad ones; there are many good people, but also some bad guys; there are gentlemen as well as base person. There are noblemen but also villains. As far as people's subjective wishes are concerned, everyone wants to stay close to gentleman and away from the villains. But in reality, things often go contrary to our wishes, sometimes we encounter bad karma, bad people and villains. Then what should we do?

The bad karma, the bad guys and the villains are the retribution of good or bad karmas we planted in the past or present life, therefore we often say "retribution in afterlife and retribution in this life". But how do we distinguish between retributions in afterlife and in this life? Tell you, the Skynet is wide and tight without a loss. It is not that there is no the retribution, just because the time has not come yet, and when the time arrives, retribution will fall upon corresponding people. This is the way of the truth.

The way of truth is not a question of whether you believe or not, it is a question of the people's perception and recognition of it. Those people who recognize truth will naturally work hard on the cause and plant good karma, so they will definitely gain good results; however, those people who don't recognize truth will act following their nature and plant evil seeds unknowingly, so they will certainly have their retribution fallen upon them. This is called, "The Tao follows the nature."

The key to the issue is why we should be grateful to the bad karma, the bad guys and the villains? The bad karma is made by us in our previous life and this life. When it comes, we should accept it with pleasure, treat it in a kind way, put an end to this bad karma and it will turn into good karma in future. This is called "turning bad karma into good karma".

There are two kinds of cases in which the bad guys are encountered by you, firstly your previous karma and consequential retribution, then your willingness to call. Someone wishes to achieve success. the greater the willingness, the greater the hardships . If you want to do well, you must pass the magic test. Bad guys provide opportunities for enhancing your kindness,

intelligence, virtue and ability. The Base persons are not kind-hearted. In reality they often look for your soft ribs and loopholes, so base persons become a pair of eyes that supervise you, so you will be perfected continuously with the help of base persons. The villains are not good, in reality they usually find your soft ribs and loopholes, so the villain become a pair of eyes to supervise you, so you will continue to improve with the help of them.

Therefore, all successes result from the convergence of karmas. At this time, we can appreciate that the good and the bad are equal in front of success. And there's no difference between the good and the bad, gentlemen and villains have difference in behavior but not in aspect of achievement.

Be grateful for all karmas! Incomparably sincere gratitude! Pure and good thanksgiving!

Gratitude not mingled with selfishness! Gratitude for all with the bosom of winner!

74

我的红木家具情
My redwood furniture

百种故事，寄物于情、情思万种

Their hundreds of stories and endow them
with all kinds of sentiments

多年前，当我第一次走进红木家私的展厅时，我站在由酸枝老料，大、小叶紫檀做成的办公家具面前，一时间，那种无形的摄受力让我不得不停下脚步，细细端详、慢慢品味……

越看越美，越看越喜欢，越触摸越不舍得离去。

酸枝老料和大、小叶紫檀这三种红木色泽安静、稳重内敛，用手触摸它的感觉如肌肤般光滑柔润，没有任何涂层，无需任何颜料的粉饰，只经人工细细打磨，就呈现了眼前这慢慢品味之后直接映入心田的感觉。据悉，酸枝和紫檀成材造器的时间需要五百年甚至上千年。天哪，这是怎样的生长历程！五百年，经受多少天地日月之精华，多少次风雨中的飘摇，多少回炎炎烈日的熏烤？这千百年天地造化的品质，在工匠们的手里，无论怎样地被切割成块，之后再组合成形状各异的家具，前后经无数道工序的破壁，都无法破灭它千百年锻造的生命气息。于是它像注入了灵魂般不动不摇、内敛大气、含蓄、端庄、典雅。

它以不言不语的方式走进你的心灵深处，和你无数次地轻声对话:《红楼》《三国》《水浒》，梅、兰、竹、菊四君子。虽然只一家具，我看见了它坚韧中的柔情似水，无声中的甜言蜜语。当手握扶手的瞬间，它所传递的不仅仅是江河湖海、万里波涛，还有多少年风中的摇曳、雨中的挺拔和烈日下的逍遥。有声时，势如破竹般令你惊叹不已，这是它成器之后唯一的声响，这声响足以惊醒你的灵魂。

红木家具来之不易，风吹过、雨淋过、烈日熏烤过，走过千百年的路。常人虽读不出它那宁静中的厚重与深沉，端庄中的诗情画意，以及典雅中的灵性交感，但仅凭它的外表就足以让俗人爱、文人亲，让有品味之人沉醉其中，享受万千风景、百种故事，寄物于情、情丝万种。

我感叹于这被风雨洗涤过的灵魂，哪里是金钱所能量化的，这经久不衰的魅力含蓄而深沉、素雅而大气、内敛而超凡脱俗!

Years ago, when I first walked into the exhibition hall of the redwood furniture, I stood in front of the office furniture made of old mahogany, big leaf sandalwood and lobular red sandalwood. I was immediately attracted by their invisible force. I had to stop to observe them carefully and appreciate them slowly...

The more I looked at them, the more beautiful they were; the more I touched them, the more I was unwilling to leave.

The colors of the three kinds of redwoods, i.e. old mahogany, big leaf sandalwood and lobular red sandalwood, are respectively quiet, stable and steady. Touching them with hand, I felt smooth and soft like skin. Without any decoration with coating or paint, only

by artificial fine grinding, it shows the feeling to fully display their charm in front of me touching deeply after slow appreciation. It is reported that the time for the furniture establishment of mahogany and sandalwood will take five hundred years or even thousands of years. Oh, how marvelous their growth process is! Five hundred years, they must have absorbed tremendous essence of the universe and undergone numerous days swaying in wind and rain as well as roasting and smoking under scorching sun over their longtime growth? The quality of the thousands of years of heaven and earth, in the hands of the craftsmen, no matter how cut into pieces, and then assembled into a variety of different shapes of furniture, Before and after the numerous improvements and breakthroughs in the processes, that still can not destroy the flavor of life that had been forged for thousands of years. So it is like a soul that is immobile, introverted, decent, implicit, dignified, elegant.

They go deep into your soul without any word and talk gently with you in countless times about the *Red Chamber*, *Three Kingdoms*, *Water Margin*, plum, orchid, bamboo, chrysanthemum, gentleman. Though they're only pieces of furniture, I sense the tenderness behind their tenacity as well as sweet words in silence. At the moment when I hold on to their handrails, they not only convey rivers, lakes, seas and miles of waves to me, but also their numerous

flickering sways in wind, tall and straight in the rain and leisure under the scorching sun over hundreds of years of their growth. When there is a sound, they will display a formidable force that you will marvel at. This is the only sound after their achievements. Such sound is enough to awaken your soul.

The redwood furniture is hard-won. They have to undergo thousands of years of growth during which they will be blown by wind, drenched by rain and scorched by the sun. Ordinary people cannot read the thick and deep in their serenity, the poetic feelings in dignity, and the spiritual sense in elegance, However, only their appearance is already enough for common people to love them, for men of letters to be intimate with them and for appreciators to indulge in them and enjoy their thousands of sceneries, their hundreds of stories and endow them with all kinds of sentiments.

I sigh at the soul baptized by the wind and rain. Such soul cannot be quantifed with money. Such everlasting charm is impliat, deep, elegant, introverted and extrodinay!

75

感悟"功德"
Perceive the "Merit and Virtue"

功德是成就我们一切美好愿望的能力

The merit and virtue are the ability to
achieve all our good wishes

昨天下午五点，结束了禅道商学院第十八期"精诚计划"的课程。这期课程收获很大，其中在攀登好汉坡的途中给了我很大的启发。

看见功德二字，我想大多数人都能明白其大概的意思，但要做更深入的理解可能就有些困难了。在此，我将自己所证悟的一点心得和体会分享给大家。

功德是成就我们一切美好愿望的能力。那什么是功，什么是德，两者之间有着什么样的关系？功就是人通过长期而不间断的努力所具备的技术才能，也就是我们的生存本领。那怎样才能实现技术才能的价值呢？在现实中，我们不乏看见有的人的确具备聪明才智，也的确有一身过人的技术，但终生怀才不遇、一事无成。什么原因呢？人所具备的聪明才智和技术本领是功，但如果只具备功而忽略了德的培养，这时的功是不具备力量的。

我打个比方：一个人或者是一家企业，在攀登山峰的路上，我们的目标一定是要到达顶峰。在此，我把人比喻成功，把山比喻成德，如果在攀登的过程中，我们只顾攀爬，心中只想尽快到达山顶，当有一天我们终于到达山顶了，这时我们面临着什么？在我们脚下已无路可走，唯一的路就是下山，这就是功的结果。如果我们知道德的重要性，我们就不会是现在的遭遇了，我们可以一边修功（不停地攀登），一边修德（不间断地把山垒得更高、再更高），于是我们攀登的高度才能是无限的。所以想要成就未来，功、德缺一不可。

看到这里，或许有人会想，我福报大，我不用修功。首先福报不是功德，功是我们的智慧才能、我们的禅定、我们的持戒、我们

的读经等等，这都是无法给予别人的，功德一定是自己修得的。而福报是可以给予和被给予的，比如我们可以用财富去帮助别人，别人也可以用财富来帮助我们。

千万别忘了：功德里面有福报，而福报里面没有功德，功德是长久的，福报是短暂的。

The courses of the 18th "Jing Cheng Plan" of Zen Tao Business School were ended at 5:00 p.m. yesterday. I have benefited a lot from this course. In particular, I was greatly enlightened on the way to climbing Haohan Slope.

Seeing the words of the merit and virtue, I think most people can understand the general meanings of them, but it may be difficult to have their deeper understanding. Hereby, I want to share a bit of my perception with you.

The merit and virtue are the ability to achieve all our good wishes. So what is merit and what is virtue? What is the relationship between the two? The "merit" is the technical ability that the people have gained after long-term and uninterrupted efforts, that is, our ability to survive. How can we realize the value of our technical ability? In reality, we do not lack to see that some people do have wisdom, intelligence and extraordinary technique, but their talents remain unrecognized and they achieve nothing in their whole life. What's the reason? The people's wisdom, intelligence and technical skill belong to merit which is powerless if they only have "merit" but neglect the cultivation of their "virtue".

Let me make an analogy: when a person or a company is climbing a mountain, their target is to reach the summit. Hereby I compare people to "merit" and the mountain to "virtue". If we only take care of climbing and think about reaching the summit, then what are we faced with after we finally reach the summit one day? We will have no other way to go under our feet but to go down the mountain. This is the result of "merit". If we know the importance of virtue, our experience will be different. We can work on "merit" (climbing continuously) on the one hand and cultivate our "virtue" (piling up the mountain constantly) on the other hand, and then our climbing height will be unlimited. Therefore, both "merit" and "virtue" are indispensable to achieving success in the future.

Seeing this, maybe someone will think, I am blessed, I don't have to cultivate merit and virtue. First of all, the blessing is not equal to merit. The "Merit" consists of wisdom and ability. It is our meditation, our precepts, our reading classics, and so on, which can not be given to others. The "Merit" must be self-cultivation, but the blessings can give and be given. For example, we can use wealth to help others, and others can use wealth to help us.

Don't forget: There are blessings in the merits and virtue, but there is no merit and virtue in the blessings. The merit and virtue are long- lasting, and the blessings are short-lived.

秋言物语

76

感悟《易经》
Perceive the *I-Ching*

《易经》的科学性和实用性
The scientific and practical nature of the *I-Ching*

　　此次美国之行，在友人的帮助之下，我又结识了一些新的美国朋友。令人印象深刻的是，此次结识的新朋友所谈论的话题最多的就是关于《易经》，其中 Michael Jaliman（麦克·嘉里曼）是一位学养深厚的资深咨询顾问，毕业于哈佛商学院，他特地送给我一本他读了长达十多年的英文版《易经》，此书由哈佛大学出版。

　　面对眼前这本陈旧的英文版《易经》，我虽然在和麦克交流，但内心久久不能平静。几十年来，我们绝大多数中国人都把国粹《易经》视为不解之谜而放弃阅读，更有人视之为迷信而轻视，但远在国外的一些人却在孜孜不倦地研究《易经》。关于《易经》，我想在此谈一谈自己一点粗浅的认识。

《易经》于六千年前为伏曦所作，他以"－－"（阴）、"－"（阳）之理阐述了与人类相关的八种物象，用八卦来表示，从而告诉人类应该遵守规矩，持守自然法则。

之后，周朝时期，纣王暴虐无道，百姓无辜受苦。在遭受纣王迫害之时，周文王用他毕生积累的实践智慧，用卦辞和爻辞分别加以注解，从而逃避了纣王的迫害，推广了宇宙秩序的观念，使人们对天人合一有了更进一步的了解。

五百年之后，孔子又在周文王的基础上，把宇宙秩序和人生规律更加紧密地联接起来，并且强调了道德实践的重要性。于是，"天行健，君子以自强不息；地势坤，君子以厚德载物"，这便是孔子"十翼"的重大意义。

《易经》讲天人合一的智慧。天人合一是什么意思，天是什么？天无形无相、无色无味、无边无际，我们所看见的蓝天白云只是漂浮在天空中的物质现象。因此，古之圣人告诉我们"天乃道也"。《易经》讲天、人、地三才之理。天人合一是自然与人和谐共处，自然界所有的物质变化都是宇宙间阴阳互动、交感，天与人相互联动所产生的宇宙万象。

《易经》对未来的预测是通过"象""数""理"的连锁作用来掌握未来的变化，从而寻求趋吉避凶的有效途径。"象""数""理"就是通过现象和数据的分析，使我们可以从中知道事物变化的结果。这正是《易经》的科学性和实用性。

During my trip to the United States, I met some new American friends with the help of my friends. The most impressive is that the new friends I made during the trip were frequently talking about the Book of *Changes*. Among these friends, Michael Jaliman is a well-educated senior consultant who graduated from the Business School of Harvard University. He especially sent me an English version of the Book of *Changes* which has read for more than a decade. This Book was published by Harvard University.

With this old English version of the Book of *Changes* in hand, I experienced no peace while talking with Michael. While I was talking to Mike, my mind was not calm for a long time. For decades, most of the Chinese people have regarded the Book of *Changes* as an unexplainable mystery and abandoned reading. Some people even treat it as superstition and despise it. But some people far abroad are studying on the Book of *Changes* with perseverance. I would like to talk about my own superficial understanding here on the Book of *Changes*.

The Book of *Changes* was written by Fu Xi six thousand years ago. In this book, he elaborated the eight kinds of object images related to human beings with "yin" (–) and "yang" (-), which are expressed in the Eight Diagrams, thus telling human beings they should follow the rules and obey the laws of the nature.

Later, during the Zhou Dynasty, the King Zhou of Shang was tyrannical without justice and the people were innocent and suffered. At the time of being persecuted by the King Zhou of Shang, King Wen of Zhou, being Xibo Marquis then, was oppressed by King Zhou. King Wen of Zhou annotated the Eight Diagrams with the hexagram words and the lines separately with his practical wisdom accumulated throughout his life, so that he escaped from the oppression of King Zhou in the end, and popularizing the idea of the order of the universe, so that people have a better understanding of the unity of heaven and man.

Five hundred years later, Confucius further combined the universal order and human rules on the basis of the theory of King Wen of

Zhou, and emphasized the importance of moral practice. Therefore, "As nature's movement is ever vigorous, so must a gentleman keep improving himself; as the earth is strong and vast, so must a gentleman be generous and tolerant to bear all things". This is where the great significance of "Ten Wings" of Confucius lies.

The *I-Ching* tells the wisdom of the unity of the Heaven and man. So what is the meaning of the harmony between the heaven and man? And what is the heaven? The heaven is invisible, colorless, tasteless, and boundless. The blue sky and the white cloud floating in the air are merely physical phenomena we see with our eyes. Therefore, the ancient saints told us that "The heaven is Tao". I-Ching tells the truth of the universe, people and the earth. The unity of the nature and man is the harmonious coexistence of the nature and man. All material changes in the nature are the cosmic images created during the interactions and the sympathy between Yin and Yang in the universe, and the inter-linkages between the heaven and human.

The *I-Ching* predicts the future by commanding the future changes through the chain reactions of image, number, and theory so that the effective approaches can be figured out to pursue good fortune and avoid disasters. Through analyzing the phenomena and data of the "image", "number", and "theory", we can know the results of changes. This is the scientific and practical nature of the Book of *Changes*.

77

实践出真知
True knowledge comes from practice

只有去实践，我们才会有认知和感悟
Only by practicing,
can we have cognition and insight

人为何而生，为何而死，生从何来，死向何去，这些问题有多少人想过，又有多少人找到了答案？

人因无明而生，因无明而死。无明即不明真理，就是不明白宇宙人生到底是怎么回事，其真正的状态和形象是怎样的。于是，我们只能顺着人的欲望所思所行，于善恶中产生和造就这个阴阳对半、好坏交错、祸福同行、苦乐共存的人类社会。顺着这样的轨迹，我们生死相续，永无休止。

生从爱欲中来，爱欲使人独自往来，独生独死，无人能代替我们的生死。从母体出来，呼吸就是我们自己的事了，因此生是死之

始，死是生之初。生死是常态，但其灵魂的归宿各不相同。说到灵魂，或许很多人都会不相信，但不相信的人也不会公开宣布"我是一个没有灵魂的人"。就算有人敢宣布，如果将其放进太平间，和所有的尸体同眠，这人不会恐惧吗？恐惧难道不是源于灵魂吗？

所以，由于我们的妄想分别执着，一件件原本美好的事情变成一件件被苦恼纠缠不休的事情。由于不明真理，我们找不到事情的根源，我们就这样不明不白地活着。

人因何而爱，因何而被爱，这些现象的根源我们想过吗？人类所面临的无数种疑惑都在经典中有答案，都在经典中有解决的方法。我们所面临的各种错综复杂的问题，在我们老祖宗的智慧里都可以得到解决，但遗憾的是我们很多人不知道，而不知道的原因是我们思想存在障碍。所以我们要清楚一切问题都必须静下心来，清净身心，通过智慧的人告诉我们的方法去实践。只有去实践，我们才会有认知和感悟，有深层次的了解，进而看清宇宙人生的本来面目。

How many people have thought about it, and how many have found the answers to the questions of why we live, why we die, where does life come from, and where does the death go?

People live by the ignorance, and die by the ignorance. The ignorance is the absence of the truth of the universe, that is, it does not understand what is going on in the universe. What is its true state and image? As a result, we can only follow our desires and create the human society of half Yin and half Yang, in the opposite direction, where there are both the good and the bad intertwined, the blessings and misfortune, and joy and sorrow coexist. Following this trajectory, we live and die, never ending.

L ife comes from the desire of love. And desires enable people to come and go alone. They live and die alone; no other people can ever live or die for us. From the moment we are born, breathing is our own business, so life is the beginning of death, death is the beginning of life. Life and death are normal phenomena, but the ascriptions of their souls are different. Speaking of the soul, perhaps many people will not believe in soul, but they would never announce that "I am a person without soul." Even if someone dares to announce it, if he is put into the mortuary and sleeps with all the bodies, will this person not be afraid? Isn't the fear from the soul?

T herefore, due to our delusions, differentiations, and obsessions, things which are originally beautiful become ones that frustrate us. Because we don't know the truth, we cannot find the roots of the matter. So we live in obscurity.

W hy do people love and why they are loved? Have we thought about the roots of these phenomena? There are answers and solutions in classics for countless doubts that human beings face. The intricate problems we face now can be solved with the help of the wisdom of our ancestors. But unfortunately many of us don't know, and the reason why we don't know is that we have obstacles in our mind. Therefore, we should know that we can only solve the problems while settling down and clearing our bodies and minds and practice the methods provided by the intelligent people. Only by practicing, can we have cognition and insight, deep understanding, and then see the true features of the universe and the life.

78

明了因果，把握人生

Know the cause and effect, control the emotions

只有真正地明了因果，才能真正地把握好自己的人生

Only by truly understanding the cause
and effect can we truly control our own life

看完电影《我不是药神》，内心受到很大冲击，感动之余，用一颗平静的心，来看待真实的人生。

我相信，每一个人对自己为什么来到人间、来做什么以及我们生命终结之时又能去到哪里等问题，都很难找到正确的答案。

影片中程勇的出现，一开始让我们看到他的穷困潦倒、家庭破裂，甚至对前妻大打出手。从这些现象中，我们能断定他是一个什么样的人呢？我想，如果没有后面的故事情节，在常人的眼光里，普遍都会认为，这是一个无所作为、性格粗暴、毫无修养的社会下层人士，总之对他的印象不会太好。

影片中的另一个人物，那个在屠宰场工作的黄毛少年，用抢劫的方式把救命的药拿到手之后，同时分发给几个慢粒白血病患者……

随着故事情节的发展，我们不难发现，程勇作为一个真实的男人，他用充满善良的、无私无畏的英雄本色行为，实现了他一开始所说的："上帝说了，救人一命胜造七级浮屠"，"上帝说了，你（我）不入地狱谁入地狱"。尽管这两句话都是佛说的，其实无论是上帝说的还是佛说的，都无关紧要，重要的是程勇从一开始的被迫赚钱，到后来的慈悲善良、无私无畏的行为，表现出他"无我、利他"之心。同时，黄毛少年也以其大无畏的"利他"之心、以其年轻的生命为代价，谱写了同样一首"利他"的生命赞歌。

这是人生的最高境界，这就是真佛在世。程勇五年的牢狱之灾、黄毛少年的生命代价，备受社会关注，国家也因此将"格列宁"

列入医保，使其从天价到平价，换来了无数人的生命再造，这就是"我不入地狱谁入地狱"的真实写照。

对以上两位可亲可敬的人物形象，我想说的是：我们不可以以貌取人，我们不可以以人的某些不良行为或表现而对人盲目下定义，我们更不能轻视、小视，甚至蔑视我们自认为从事"低级"行业的人。在佛的眼里，众生平等。

佛说众生平等，即包括猪、马、牛、羊、狗在内的一切众生。所以，佛在经典中清楚地告诉我们，众生皆有佛性，我们每个人都是因不同的因缘而共同来到这个人世间，我们来了，有些事情注定就要发生，一切事情的发生都是自己的因果造就。因此，只有真正地明了因果，我们才能真正地把握好自己的人生。

After watching the movie "I am not a Drug God", I was quite impacted. Besides being touched, I started to look at the real life in peace.

I believe that it is difficult for everyone to find the right answer to the question of why they came to the world, what they do, and where we can go when our lives are over.

In the film, Cheng Yong's appearance made us see that his poverty was overwhelmed, his family was broke down, and even his ex-wife was beaten. From these phenomena, we can determine what kind of a person he is? I may wonder, without knowing the story followed, I think that if there is no story behind it, in the eyes of ordinary people, it is generally believed that this is a low-level person who is inaction, rude with no accomplishment or self-cultivation. In short, people have no good impression on him whatsoever.

Another character in the film, the yellow-haired boy who worked in a slaughter house. He robbed the life-saving medicine, and distributed it to several patients with chronic myeloid leukemia...

With the development of the storyline, it is not difficult to find out that Cheng Yong, is a true man in real life. He achieved what he has said at the beginning, with his kindness and his selfless and heroic behaviors: "God said, saving one life earns more merits than building a pagoda of seven stories." And he also said, "As God says, I don't go to hell and who goes to hell? " Although these two sentences are all Buddhism, in fact, neither what God said or what the Buddha said isirrelevant. What is important is that Cheng Yong was forced to make money from the beginning, and later to be compassionate, benevolent, selfless and fearless. He showed his mind of "selfless, altruism". At the same time, the Huang Mao boy also wrote the same "altruism" life hymn with his fearless "altruism" at the expense of his young life.

This is the highest realm of life, and this is the true Buddha in the mortal world. Cheng Yong's five years of imprisonment and the cost of Huang Mao's young life have attracted the attention of the society. The country has therefore included "Gleeve" in medical insurance, from the sky-high price to the parity, in exchange for the re-creation of countless people's lives. It is a true portrayal of "If I don't go to hell and who goes to hell?"

From the above two respectable figures, I especially want to say: We can't take people by appearance. We can't blindly define people with certain bad behaviors or performances. Moreover, we can not despise, ignore or even look down upon those we think who are engaged in the "low-level" industry. All beings are equal in the eyes of Buddha.

The Buddha said that all the people are equal, that is, all sentient beings including pigs, horses, cattle, sheep and dogs, etc. Therefore, the Buddha clearly tells us in the classics that all beings have buddha nature. Everyone of us comes to the world for different causes. And we come to the world, some things are bound to happen, everything happens for its own causes. Therefore, only by truly understanding the cause and effect can we truly control our own life.

79

点滴处见修养、德行和品质
Seeing cultivation, virtue and quality at everywhere

事不大，但点滴中蕴含着修养、德行和品质

It's not a big deal, but it embodies cultivation,
virtue and quality

今天，我从办公室所在楼层 36 楼乘电梯到 31 楼处理工作时，由于正值午餐时段，电梯比较拥挤，当我和另一位同事进入电梯时，我发现旁边一位身形微胖的青年男士双手紧抱双臂，一双温和的眼睛和略带微笑的嘴角，使他整张脸看上去都充满善意。可以看出他之所以双手抱臂，一是怕挤到别人，二是想让自己尽量少占用空间以方便旁边的人。我下电梯时还不禁回头看了他一下，发现他的着装不属于公司员工的，于是我在想，这样一副带着微笑、充满善意的表情其实是一种无声的温馨。从这一现象，我不禁想起在纽约时一些相同的场面。

美国纽约，这个世界知名的发达城市，在那里我们看见的大多数人，无论是从事服务行业，如超市收银、打扫卫生以及其他服务

型工作，还是被服务的对象，无论在哪里的电梯里碰到，他们都会很友善地和我们打招呼。这种现象在纽约随处可见，这是什么原因导致的呢？

与此同时，我们还看见在整容还没有风行的年代，很多和善的人都气质脱俗、五官端正、身材高挑（女）、体格健壮（男），这又是什么原因导致的呢？

世间万象皆有因缘，我们从佛家的经典之中不难看出，"三十二相，八十种好"，即指人的相貌有三十二种，其中就有八十种好的地方。一个人尊贵的气质和良好的相貌都源自于福报，而福报又源自于生生世世的修养和行善积德。

因此，同样一张笑脸，一双充满善意和喜悦的眼睛，一句友好的问候，真的能让人感到温暖。事不大，但点滴中蕴含着修养、德行和品质。

Today, I took the elevator down to the 31st floor from the 36th floor of my office to handle some work there. As it was lunch time, the elevator was a little crowded. When I and another colleague entered the crowded elevator, I noticed a chubby young man at side clasping his arms with his hands. A pair of mild eyes and a slightly smiling mouth made his whole face look friendly. It could be seen that he clasped his arms in order to avoid squeezing others and make himself occupy as little space as possible to facilitate the people around him. When I got off the elevator, I couldn't help but look back at him and found that his dress was not those of my company's employees. Therefore, I thought that such a friendly smile was actually kind of silent warmth. From this phenomenon, I can't help but think of some of the same scenes in New York.

New York, a world-famous developed city, where most of the people we see, whether in the service industry, such as supermarket cashiers, cleaning, and other service-oriented jobs, while some people are served objects. Whenever we meet any people in the elevator, they will greet us very kindly. This phenomenon can be seen everywhere in New York. What is the reason for this?

At the same time, we also saw that in the age when cosmetic surgery was not popular, many good people were temperamental, well- rounded, tall (female), and physically strong (male). What's the reason for this?

Everything in the world has its own karma. We can learn easily from the Buddhist scriptures that "thirty-two looks and eighty marks", that is, there are thirty-two kinds of people's appearance, of which there are eighty good places. A person's noble temperament and good looks originated from blessings which came from cultivation, doing the good and accumulating virtue generation after generation.

Therefore, the same smile face, a pair of eyes full of kindness and joy, a friendly greeting, can really make people feel warm. It's not a big deal, but it embodies cultivation, virtue and quality.

80

打破束缚，选择人生
Break the bondage and choose life

家是世间一切方法的根本，也是爱和被爱的束缚之地

Family is fundamental for all methods in the world
but also the restrained place for all love and being loved

道生天地，天地生万物，万物之灵，人也。人从哪里来？人从轮回中来，父精母血合和而构成了人这一胎生动物。一句话，人都是父母所生，这是因缘决定的，我们无法选择父母，但我们一定可以选择人生。

既然人是父母所生，那就一定有家，家是世间一切方法的根本，也是一切爱和被爱的束缚之地。夫妻之爱、父母之爱、儿女之爱，在给我们温暖和幸福的同时，也给我们带来各种各样不舒服的感受。于是家便成了我们观"诸法无常"，体会喜怒哀乐无常变化的根本之地。

说到这里，我想起那位网络上被称为"全中国最帅和尚"的释明心法师。我和法师结缘有四年时间，接触交谈中，同样发现他之

所以出家是因为观到了家庭的无常变化，以及他在工作单位所感受到的种种不舒服，使他产生了出离心。与此同时，选择出家，法师又怕伤及父母的爱心和期盼心，于是法师善巧而为，通过考取佛学院而顺理成章地出家了。这是明心法师出家的大概情况。

我在想，出家其实也是不舒服的，和在家一样的不舒服。寺庙也是无常烦恼苦，于是又一种出离心产生了。这时，心要从自己的身体出离，身体也是一个家，我们的心要从这个家里走出来，才能够真正解脱。心怎么才能走出身体呢？

我们身体所具备的六根：眼、耳、鼻、舌、身、意，遇到六尘时就产生了色、声、香、味、触、法。人在六根和六尘中产生了六种结果：烦、恼、忧、悲、伤、苦。所以要想真正解脱，必须明白身体这个家的真相。让心从身体中走出来，首先要看明白身体是一个被污染的家，家里屎尿具足，生命不会长久，只有忘掉身体，进入无我、利他之境界，才能到达《道德经》中所说的"吾有大患，及吾有身；及吾无身，吾有何患"之境界。

Tao gives birth to the heaven and earth, heaven and earth produce everything, people is the spirit above all things. Where do the people come from? The people come from the reincarnation, and the father and the mother are together and constitute the human, a viviparous animal. In a word, the people are born by parents. This is a karma decision. We cannot choose parents, but we can certainly choose life.

Now that people's lives are given by their parents, there must be families. Family is fundamental for all methods in the world

but also the restrained place for all love and being loved. The love of husband and wife, the love of parents, the love of children, while giving us warmth and happiness, also bring us a variety of uncomfortable feelings. Therefore, the family has become the fundamental place for us to observe "the impermanence of all kinds of laws" and to experience the change of emotions and sorrows.

Here, I think of Master Shi Ming Xin, who is called "the most handsome monk in China" on the Internet. I have been in the relationship with the Master for four years. During the conversation, I also found out that he wanted to become a monk after observing the unusual changes in the family and various uncomfortable feelings in the working place, which caused him to be centrifuged. At the same time, choosing a monk, the Master is afraid of hurting his parents' love and expectation, and then he skillfully realized his purpose by being admitted by Buddhist College. This is the general situation of Master Ming Xin's being a monk.

I am thinking that it is uncomfortable to be a monk, just as being at home. The temple's life is also full of changes and troubles, so another kind of centrifugal is produced. At this time, the soul must escape from the body, the body is also a home, and our soul must come out of this house to really realize the liberation. How can the soul get out of the body?

There are six sense organs in our body: eyes, ears, nose, tongue, body and mind, when it encounters the six dusts, it generates color, sound, flavor, taste, touch and law. The people have six kinds of results in six roots and six dusts: annoyance, irritation, worry, sadness, injury, and suffering. Therefore, if you want to be truly free, you must understand the truth about the body home. To escape from your body, you must take the body as a polluted home. the home is full of urine, the life will not last long. Only forget the body, enter the realm of selfless, altruism, can you realize the state mentioned in the *Tao Te Ching*: "We have fears because we have a self. When we do not regard that body as self, what have we to fear?" "I have a great trouble, because I have a body; If I have no body, what am I suffering?"

81

成就他人，方可成就自己

Help others, achieve your meaning of life

天地万物都是因缘所致

Everything in heaven
and earth is caused by karma

我们几乎都会看到这样的一个现象，出生只有一百天左右的宝宝，在和同龄宝宝一起玩耍时都会相互争夺玩具，这一行为是不教而会的一种天性。

　　所谓天性，其实就是人在生生世世的轮回中，由善恶行为的因素所产生在当下的现象。比如有人天生拥有一副好嗓子，有人天生丽质，有人天生擅文，有人天生擅理，这些都是我们在过去一生中所修习的结果。总之，天地万物都是因缘所致。

　　但非常遗憾的是由于受尘垢的污染，我们忘记了自己的本性，失去了认识自己的能力。我们看自己就像站在一面布满污垢的镜子面前，所看到的并不是自己的真实面目。我们被假象迷惑了，认为那个充满污垢的镜子里的人就是自己，于是我们对自己的认识产生了莫大的偏差。这种偏差导致我们在做人做事时颠倒梦想，以假为真，以真为假。

　　例如，我们把"人不为己，天诛地灭"这句话，理解为人都是自私的，人如果不自私就不会去创造，于是就会遭天报。大错特错！在此，我想举例说明，讲一个从小听到大的故事：一个母亲非常疼爱自己的儿子，从小到大，母亲都不辞辛苦地满足儿子所有的需求。后来，儿子长大了，需求也更大了，母亲满足不了，儿子便开始以不正当的手段骗取财物，最终因抢劫杀人而走上了一条不归之路。在行刑枪决时，儿子要求再喝一口母亲的奶，于是儿子用坚硬的牙齿咬掉了母亲的乳头，这是儿子临死前对母亲溺爱的仇恨。这就是"人不为己，天诛地灭"的真实写照。

　　发生这一事件的原因，在于我们认识的颠倒，母亲总以为满足儿子的愿望就是爱，母亲这些行为既没有为儿子着想，也没有为自己着想。母亲根本就不懂得，当坏事做到一定数量的时候，灾难就会降临。这还不是最可怕的，更为可怕的是那个被枪决的儿子，到死都没明白"人不为己，天诛地灭"的道理。而这位可怜的母亲，在儿子临死前咬掉自己乳头之后，应该明白是自己害了儿子。

"人不为己，天诛地灭"，所有的利己都是建立在利他基础之上的，正所谓"圣人无私，而成其私"，我们翻开历史的记载，从古至今就没有任何一个自私自利的人能成就一番大业。实言：要想实现自己好的梦想，先去成就别人，方可成就自己。

We almost always see the phenomenon that a baby born only about a hundred days or so will compete for toys when playing with a baby of the same age. This behavior is an instinct that is not taught.

The so-called instinct is actually the current phenomenon generated by the factors of the good and evil behaviors of the people in the reincarnations of their generations. For example, some people are born to have a good voice or beautiful appearance; some good at arts while others good at mathematics, all of which are cultivated results in our previous generations. In short, everything in heaven and earth is caused by karma.

But unfortunately, because we are polluted by dirt, we have forgotten our own nature and we have lost our ability to know ourselves. We see ourselves as standing in front of a mirror full of dirt. What we see is not our true face. We are confused by illusions. We think that the person in the mirror full of dirt is myself, so we have a great deviation from our own understanding. This deviation leads us to reverse our dreams when we are doing things, false for true, true for false.

For example, we will interpret the phrase "Every man for himself, and the devil takes the hindmost". that people are all selfish. If they are not selfish, they will not create, and will be punished by heaven. It is absolutely wrong! Here, I would like to give an example to tell a story that I heard from the young to the elder: A mother loved her son very much. From the baby to growing up, the mother had worked tirelessly

to meet all her son's needs. Later, when the son grew up, his demand was even greater. The mother could not satisfy, the son began to illegally cheat and finally be sentenced to death for killing people in rubbery. At the time of the execution, the son asked for suckling his mother another milk the last time before being shot, but he bit off his mother's nipple with his tough teeth. It was the hatred of the son towards the doting mother before his death. And it is also the true portrait of this phrase: "Every man for himself, and the devil takes the hindmost".

The reason for this incident is that our cognition is upside down for this case. The mother always thinks that the love is to satisfy her son's desire. The mother's behavior is neither for her son nor for her own sake. The mother does not know at all that the disaster will come when the evil deeds are accumulated to certain number. This is not the most terrible. What is even more terrible is that the son who was shot down did not understand the words: "Every man for himself, and the devil takes the hindmost." And the poor mother, after the son gnawed his nipple before his death, finally knew that she had hurt her son.

"Every man is for himself, and the devil takes the hindmost." All self interests are all based on benefiting others. It is so called "A saint is selfless, but accomplish his private desires". We open the record of history. No selfish people could accomplish great success from the ancient time on. To be honest: if you want to realize your own dream, firstly you make others successful and then you may unexpectedly find your demands met.

图书在版编目（CIP）数据

秋言物语 / 马小秋著. --北京：社会科学文献出
版社，2019.2（2019.6重印）
ISBN 978-7-5201-4268-7

Ⅰ.①秋⋯ Ⅱ.①马⋯ Ⅲ.①资产管理公司－企业管
理－经验－深圳 Ⅳ.①F832.39

中国版本图书馆CIP数据核字（2019）第016867号

秋言物语

著　　者 / 马小秋

出 版 人 / 谢寿光
项目统筹 / 邓泳红　吴　敏
责任编辑 / 吴　敏　张　媛

出　　版 / 社会科学文献出版社·皮书出版分社（010）59367127
　　　　　　地址：北京市北三环中路甲29号院华龙大厦　邮编：100029
　　　　　　网址：www.ssap.com.cn
发　　行 / 市场营销中心（010）59367081　59367083
印　　装 / 三河市东方印刷有限公司

规　　格 / 开　本：787mm×1092mm 1/16
　　　　　　印　张：20.75　字　数：241千字
版　　次 / 2019年2月第1版　2019年6月第4次印刷
书　　号 / ISBN 978-7-5201-4268-7
定　　价 / 98.00元

本书如有印装质量问题，请与读者服务中心（010-59367028）联系